Herbert Lockwood Willett

The prophets of Israel

Herbert Lockwood Willett

The prophets of Israel

ISBN/EAN: 9783743358591

Manufactured in Europe, USA, Canada, Australia, Japa

Cover: Foto ©Lupo / pixelio.de

Manufactured and distributed by brebook publishing software (www.brebook.com)

Herbert Lockwood Willett

The prophets of Israel

The Prophets of Israel

BY

Herbert L. Willett, Ph. D.

*tant Professor in Semitic Languages and Literatures in the
University of Chicago.*

Christian Board of Publication
St. Louis, Mo.

PREFATORY NOTE

No apology need be offered for departing from Archbishop Usher's chronology, which has long been recognized as unsatisfactory by biblical students. The dates given in this book are those commonly regarded as approximately correct. The outlines of the prophetic books follow the chapters in which they are considered, and form a brief syllabus for their further study. The questions are intended as an aid to the reader in fixing in the memory the contents of each chapter. The references are uniformly to the Revised Version. Suggestions regarding literature will be found at the end of the book, and there is appended a table showing the synchronization of the prophetic work with political events.

H. L. W.

The National Convention of the Disciples of Christ, held in Springfield, Illinois, October 16-23, 1896, adopted the following recommendations:

"1. That this convention approve the idea of adding, within certain limits, the educational feature to the Christian Endeavor Societies among us. This added educational feature shall include helps for the systematic reading of the Bible, a selected course of reading concerning missions in general, and our own missions in particular, and thorough instruction as to the origin, the principles, and the history of our own movement for the restoration of New Testament Christianity.

"2. That this convention approve of the purpose to provide a series of hand-books for our young people covering the fields not already satisfactorily covered."

CONTENTS

CHAPTER   PAGE

I. General Features of Prophecy . . 11
II. The Messages of the Prophets . . 19
III. The Beginnings of Prophecy—Moses and Samuel 27
IV. Elijah and Elisha 36
V. Amos, the Prophet of Righteousness . 44
VI. Hosea, the Prophet of Divine Love . 53
VII. Isaiah: the Prophet as a Statesman . 63
VIII. Micah, the Tribune of the People . 75
IX. The Prophecies of Nahum, Zephaniah Habakkuk and Obadiah . . . 81
X. Jeremiah, the Martyr Prophet . . 93
XI. Ezekiel, the Shepherd of the Exiles . 105
XII. The Evangelical Prophecy . . . 115
XIII. Haggai and Zechariah, the Prophets of the Revival of Jerusalem . . . 128
XIV. Later Prophetic Books—Malachi, Joel, Jonah and Daniel 137
XV. The Messianic Hope 147
Bibliography 154
Chronological Tables . . . 155-156

"The Lord thy God will raise up unto thee a prophet from the midst of thee, of thy brethren, like unto me; unto him shall ye hearken. "When therefore the people saw the signs which he did, they said, This is of a truth the prophet that cometh into the world."

—Deut. 18: 15. John 6: 14.

The Prophets of Israel

CHAPTER I

GENERAL FEATURES OF PROPHECY

1. Israel was a prophet nation. It was chosen to be the messenger of God to the world. It was not a selection for favor, but for service. There was no other way of revealing divine truth save through a people in whom, or at least in some of whom, it could become incarnate. Israel was selected, not because it was the most enlightened or advanced in civilization, but because it was most plastic and impressionable. As Jesus passed by the Scribes and Pharisees because they were too fixed in their ideas to be used by Him, and chose the fishermen for His disciples, so Israel was chosen to be the herald nation because it had least to unlearn. This process of selection is recorded in that book of the Old Testament which deals with the beginnings of history, and especially of Israel's history. Of the three sons of Noah, Shem was chosen, and received his father's prophetic promise that in his tents God should dwell (Gen. 9:26, 27). Still later Abram was selected from among the Semitics, that through his posterity the nations of

the earth should be blessed (Gen. 12:1-3). Similarly Jacob was designated as the one through whom the divine purpose was to be manifested (Gen. 28:10-15), and subsequently, after he had proved in some measure his fitness, he was given the name Israel, which ever after became the possession of his posterity (Gen. 32:24-28). The people thus selected had a mission to the world. That mission was not war and conquest, as with the Assyrians, nor philosophy and art, as with the Greeks, nor organization and law, as with the Romans. It was theirs rather to speak for God, to serve as the channel of the divine self-disclosure to the world. To be fitted thus to act they needed the preparation of a long education regarding the character and purposes of God. The experiences of their history were means by which this education was secured. Their laws and religious services were also aids to a knowledge of God. But the supreme agency by which they were taught was provided in the ministry of the prophets. Thus Israel, which was itself destined to be a prophet nation to the other nations of the world, was the pupil of a line of prophets, who spoke the divine will with ever increasing fullness, until their partial disclosures of God were completed by the final revelation in the Christ. The whole story of prophetic work is told in a word by the author of the Book of Hebrews in his opening sentence. "God, who at various times and in fragmentary ways, spoke in times past to the fathers in the prophets, hath in these last days spoken unto us in His Son."

2. The English word "prophet" is derived from the Greek *prophetes*, which means one who speaks forth a message. The Hebrew word ordinarily employed to describe such a person is *nabhi*, which has essentially the same meaning, with the added idea of speaking for or in behalf of another. Thus the prophet was a speaker for God, a bearer of his message. Two other words were sometimes employed—*ro'eh* and *chozeh*—both of which signify seer, almost in our sense of clairvoyant, one who sees things hidden from others.[1] But this is not the usual idea connected with prophecy, which normally moves upon a higher level of ethical or spiritual purpose. In none of these words is the idea of prediction expressed. This was, indeed, often a part of the function of a prophet, but only incidental to his real purpose as a preacher of righteousness. Nor was the prophet merely a passive instrument of the divine Spirit. That he was guided in his message and work by a power above his own is constantly affirmed; but not in the sense that he lost his individuality. He was a man whose character, either natural or as the result of his experience, made him responsive to the leadings of the Spirit of God, and

---

[1] We learn from 1 Sam. 9:9 that the word "seer" was the earlier one referring to the prophet, but denoting especially that quality whereby he was enabled to assist those in need of counsel or in search of lost property.

thus capable of interpreting both by his life and his message the divine will. The prophets were not merely men of genius, who thus became leaders of their race. No theory which omits the element of inspiration in their lives can account for the facts. They were men who wrought and spake as they were impelled by the Holy Spirit. Yet, possessing this controlling purpose, they seemingly acted with entire freedom in their choice of methods, and each maintained throughout his own characteristics.

3. Prophecy, in its general aspects, was not limited to Israel. Most nations of antiquity possessed orders of men devoted to the services of their respective religions, though such functions were not infrequently closely related to those of the priests. Among the Babylonians and Arabs the prophets had the character both of rude preachers of the national religion and of diviners. In the latter capacity they held an important place in the life of the people. In superstitious ages an auspicious occasion was sought for every enterprise, and accordingly the prophet or seer was often consulted. The forms of divination were various, such as observation of the flight of birds, inspection of the entrails of animals, shooting with arrows, consultation of teraphim (Ezek. 21:21), and watching the movement of liquid in a cup or other vessel (Gen. 44:5). The only forms of divination permitted to Israel were the sacred lot (Josh. 18:10; 1 Sam. 14:41, 42), and the urim and thummim (Ex. 28:30; 1

Sam. 28:6), the latter being used by the priest. Other ruder forms of prophetic activity are observed in the conduct of the prophets of the Phœnician god, Baal. These men resembled the modern dervishes in the methods by which they sought to obtain the regard and assistance of their deity. They shouted his name, they danced about his altar, and gashed themselves with knives, as was their custom (1 Kings 26:28). The object of these practices was, of course, to induce that physical exhaustion and unconsciousness which was generally regarded as necessary to communion with deity. Sometimes bands of prophets roamed about the country, or lived in particular localities, their "prophesying" consisting of rude and often fanatical preaching accompanied by music. Into such a circle the bystander might be drawn by the contagion of excitement, and even entirely overcome. In company with other nations of the age, Israel possessed these undisciplined and grotesque types of prophecy to a limited degree, and though the work of the true prophets of God moved upon levels far above this, yet certain features of the ruder sort manifested themselves even in the work of some of the great prophets (1 Kings 18:46; 2 Kings 3:15). The only case of true prophecy among a heathen people mentioned in the Old Testament is that of Balaam (Num. 22:24), who, though he attempted to curse Israel for a reward, was compelled to bless instead. The explanation of this exception is no doubt to be found in the relation of Balaam's message to the fortunes of the chosen people.

4. The true prophets were selected especially for the work they were to do. They were not taken at random, but were chosen because they were the men best suited to accomplish their respective tasks. This fitness was sometimes owing to their temperament or disposition; sometimes it resulted from their peculiar experiences. In either case they were those most responsive to the divine Spirit; most capable of comprehending the divine purpose, and most competent to proclaim it to the people. In most cases the prophet received a call to his work, and this call might take any one of a variety of forms, as an audible message (1 Sam. 3:8-10), a vision (Isa. 6:1), or a spiritual impulse apart from any external sign. The methods of divine communication with the prophet during his career were equally various, dreams and visions serving this purpose at times. But in the ministries of the great prophets the will of God was apprehended by that type of spiritual illumination which seemingly required neither of these media. The messenger spoke for God because he had spoken with God. His nature was open to the impress of the divine Spirit; and out of that life which he lived with God he spoke to the men of his day.

NOTE ON THE PEOPLE OF ISRAEL.—"Israel" was the name of the people descended from Jacob, and more remotely from Abraham, the first to bear the designation "Hebrew" (Gen. 14: 13). They belonged to the Semitic stock, and were closely related by

General Features of Prophecy 17

the Arabs, Assyrians, Babylonians, Aramæ-
œnicians, Moabites, Ammonites and Edom-
In national characteristics they closely
ed these other members of the group. Their
as traced to Mesopotamia (Gen. 11:28), and
ence their ancestors by migration through the
regions (Padan-Aram, Haran; Gen. 11:31;
me at last to Canaan. In the earliest period
history, while they were still a clan rather
ation, they were known as "Hebrews" (Gen.
Ex. 2:11). Later on "Israel," or "Children
l," became their usual designation, from the
t of Canaan to the disruption of the kingdom
close of Solomon's reign (Josh. 14:1; Jud.
am. 28:1; 1 Kings 11:25). After this divi-
he nation into two kingdoms (937 B. C.), the
portion, with its capital at Samaria, retained
e "Israel," while the southern was called
" from the tribe which composed the great
of its people (1 Kings 15:9; 16:29; 2 Kings
After the downfall of the kingdom of Israel
. C., Judah alone survived, and it was not
ntly the case that the word "Israel" was
by the prophets to this portion of the original
to preserve the thought of the national unity
stiny as first conceived, even though the
of that unity in its earlier form was no longer
(Jer. 17:13; Ezek. 3:7; Mal. 1:1). But
in Jeremiah's day the term "Jews," as de-
the people of Judah, was in use (Jer. 32:12),
became the usual designation in later periods,
not so much to the inhabitants of the
province alone, as to the entire nation as
ished from the Gentiles (Zech. 8:23; Neh.
th. 2:5). This is likewise the New Testa-
e of the word. The most representative of
ames was "Israel," and it is the only one
ay be properly applied to the entire people
ages of the history. The term "Prophets of
s not restricted, therefore, to those religious
whose work lay in the northern kingdom
he period of the monarchy, but describes the
ody of men who had to do with prophetic
ong the chosen people.

QUESTIONS

1. For what purpose was Israel selected? What principle determined the selection? Through what persons did the line of selection pass? What was the special mission of Israel? In what manner was the nation prepared for this work? What was the most important of the agencies employed in this preparation? 2. What are the derivation and meaning of the word "prophet"? How is the word "seer" used in the Old Testament? Was the function of prediction an essential part of the work of a prophet? Was the prophet a passive or active instrument of the divine Spirit? Was he merely a man of genius? 3. Did other nations have prophets? What two directions did their activity take? What were the different methods of divining? What methods were permitted to Israel? How did the prophets of Baal attempt to secure communion with their god? Did any of these ruder forms of prophecy have a place in Israel? What case of true prophecy in a heathen is given in the Bible? How may it be explained? 4. What determined the choice of the prophets? How was the prophet set apart to his work? In what forms, either at his call or later, did the divine message come to him? Which of these methods was most employed?

CHAPTER II

THE MESSAGES OF THE PROPHETS

1. The literature of the Old Testament includes several kinds of books. There are the legal writings, which record the laws by which the people were to regulate their conduct. Such books as Exodus, Leviticus, Numbers and Deuteronomy are of this class, though they include a framework of history in which the institutes of Israel were set. Then there are the historical books, such as Chronicles, Ezra, Nehemiah and Esther, whose purpose it is to recount the experiences of the nation at various periods in its career. Again, there are the wisdom books, or those produced by the wise men, the philosophers, the sages. They deal for the most part with the problems of practical life, and include such works as Proverbs, Job, Ecclesiastes and the Song of Songs. There are also devotional and elegiac writings, such as Psalms and Lamentations; and the Book of Daniel furnishes an example of Apocalyptic. There still remains, however, the most important section of Old Testament literature, viz., the prophetic writings. They not only constitute the largest section of Hebrew literature, but their influence was far greater than that of all the other classes combined.

2. The prophetic books were divided by

the Jews into two sections—the "Former Prophets" and the "Latter Prophets." The first of these divisions consisted of the four books which treated the history of the nation in a prophetic spirit, *i. e.*, Joshua, Judges, Samuel and Kings, the two books of Samuel, like those of Kings, being counted as one. These books, it was seen, were not mere recitals of events, such as historians would set down, but dealt apparently only with such experiences of the past as served in some measure to illustrate the divine faithfulness in spite of sin on the part of the people, and the disastrous consequences of disobedience. They are, in other words, collections of historical materials gathered out of the vast treasury of the past experiences of the nation or of individuals, and intended to emphasize the principles of righteousness which the prophets were ever concerned to teach. They seem to have constituted the messages which the prophets were constantly repeating; and thus they indicate the fact that these men were accustomed in their preaching to use material (1) from the past, in the form of narratives of conspicuous lives, like those of Samuel, David and Solomon, which afforded ample features both for imitation and warning; or in the form of particular events, or series of events in the national life, such as the conquest, the work of the judges, or the disruption of the kingdom; (2) from the present, in the form of a picture of present conditions or a reference to current events, or (3) from the future in the form of predictions general or special, near or remote. The second and third of these elements appear to only a limited extent in the writings of this group, but they are nevertheless present. A careful examination of these books will show that they do not give the entire history, but only scanty selections from it, referring the reader who is desirous of fuller details to the court or national records or to the writings of individuals (1 Kings 16:27; 2 Kings 12:19; 1 Chr. 29:29). It was their purpose rather to enforce the religious principles which found illustration in that history. Therefore, they are properly reckoned as prophetic books, their religious purpose being primary.

3. The second group of prophetic books, called the "Latter Prophets," includes the records of the work and words of particular prophets. In this group, as in the first, there were four books, viz., Isaiah, Jeremiah, Ezekiel and the Twelve. The last included the so-called "Minor Prophets," from Hosea to Malachi. These last were designated "Minor" not because they were unimportant, but because they were marked by greater brevity than characterized the three "Major Prophets." The books of this group furnish us a picture, more or less complete, of the men whose names they bear, of the times in which they lived, and of their messages. The prophets were preachers of righteousness, and these books are practically collections of their sermons, preached

wherever opportunity offered. In this preaching they are seen to have made use of the same three classes of material, viz., that from the past, that of the present and that relating to the near or remoter future. Of these the second was most used, though the first and third were often employed. As would be expected, probably few of the sermons of any one prophet have come down to us. Perhaps only those most important or most frequently delivered have been preserved. Again, we seem to have only the outlines, not the complete reports, of those which have been preserved. This seems to be true likewise of the great New Testament sermons. The prophets were primarily speakers, and their writing was only done to preserve what they had said so that it might be sent out to wider circles than could hear their voices (Jer. 30:1, 2; 36:1). Sometimes they wrote letters directed to particular persons or groups, but this method was rare (Jer. 29:1; 2 Chr. 21:12). Occasionally they resorted to symbolic means to impress their messages or to secure attention, such as giving to their children suggestive names (Hos. 1:4, 6; Isa. 7:3; 8:3), or performing some public act which was illustrative of their messages, such as erecting a tablet (Isa. 8:1), burying a linen girdle (Jer. 13:1-9), or removing furniture (Ezek. 12:1-11).

4. The message of the prophet was closely related to the age in which he lived and to the people with whom he associated. He was no abstract personality, living apart

from men, and speaking oracles which had their only significance in and for the future. The prophets were the preachers, the reformers, the incarnate conscience of their age. They spoke primarily for their own day, not for the future. They were identified with the various social classes and political parties of the time. They were often the most potent factors in directing legislation and shaping the policies of the state. They were constant disturbers of the peace to wicked or indifferent rulers. They were the most important religious forces in their times. Therefore the necessity of knowing something of the period in which a prophet lived if we would understand his work. The prophets cannot be comprehended apart from a knowledge of the circumstances in which they stood. Their ideals were lofty. They sought to raise the people to higher levels of ethical and religious life. Righteousness in the individual and in the community was of first importance. Their teachings always centered in the unity, personality and ethical character of God, and issued in a demand for conformity to His will. They taught likewise that the golden age of Israel's life was not past, but to come, and this confidence grew with the passing years into all the glory of the Messianic hope. Thus prophecy is seen to be unique in the life of Israel, moving upon levels unapproached by the prophets of other nations. The great prophets arose at crises in the national life, and in the strength and under the guidance of the divine Spirit, they braved the bitterest opposition, proclaimed fearlessly the will of God, went heroically to death if need be, and thus pointed the way to the realization of the highest ideals for the nation and the world.

5. It is probable that the writings of some of the prophets were in circulation at a period soon after their work closed, and in a few instances there are hints that fragments or small collections of the prophet's sayings were sent out during his life, to serve the purposes of popular religious instruction. It was during the exile, however, that the literary impulse became more pronounced, and doubtless in these years (586-538 B. C.) something like formal collections of prophetic writings were attempted. This process was continued in the period of Judah's revival, especially by men like Nehemiah and Ezra; and as there gradually arose the consciousness that the gift of prophecy had been withdrawn, it became a matter of increasing importance to gather all the writings which the true prophetic spirit had produced. In the formation of the collection certain portions of the literature appear to have been anonymous, and in certain instances to have been added to the writings of well-known prophets on grounds of general resemblance, similarity of theme or some kindred cause, as in the case of parts of the books of Isaiah, Zechariah, and perhaps Micah; or they were left without assignment to any writer, and took

The Messages of the Prophets 25

their name from some significant word which they contained, as in the case of "Malachi" (meaning "my messenger," Mal. 3:1). The four books of the prophets, viz., Isaiah, Jeremiah, Ezekiel and the Twelve, are mentioned in the later Jewish writings as already forming the prophetic collection as early as 180 B. C. (Ecclus. 48), and it is probable that even before this time they were recognized by the Jews as a closed body of writings, next to the five books of the Law in importance.

QUESTIONS

1. Describe the legal, historical, wisdom, devotional and apocalyptic literature of the Old Testament. What class of writings was most important? 2. Into what two divisions were the prophetic books separated? What were the Former Prophets? What was the character of these books? How do they differ from history? What three classes of material did they use? From what did they draw their information regarding the past? 3. What do the Latter Prophets include? Why were some of the books called "Minor Prophets"? What is the literary form of these books? How fully are the sermons of the prophets preserved? Why did the prophets write their messages? What other methods did they employ? 4. How are the prophetic messages related to the periods in which the prophets lived? Did they speak primarily for the present or the future? How were they regarded by evil rulers and citizens? What did they seek to accomplish? To what did they look forward? How does prophecy in Israel compare with that in other nations? Did the prophets arise in regular succession or at critical periods? What may be said of their heroism? 5. How did their writings get into circulation? What was the great literary period of the history? In what later time was the collection of prophetic writings enlarged? What

feeling added to the importance of gathering all such writings? Were there any prophetic writings whose authors were unknown? What was done with them? By what time was the list of prophetic books regarded as complete?

CHAPTER III

THE BEGINNINGS OF PROPHECY—MOSES AND SAMUEL

1. Israel's selection as a chosen people began with Abraham's call to leave his eastern home and migrate into Canaan, and yet it was not until almost the close of the period of Egyptian bondage that the national life really began, and the education of the people as called to a special mission was undertaken. Still the lives of the patriarchs are not without profound significance as evidences of a special force operating in this people, even in these earliest years. Abraham is even called a prophet on one occasion (Gen. 20:7), and though his life exhibits traits at variance with the highest ideals, yet judged by the standards of his time and the lives of his contemporaries, he is seen to have possessed those elements of trust in God and obedience which are the foundations of every great character. The lives of Isaac, Jacob and Joseph also exhibited many traits which served admirably the purposes of prophetic instruction. In them, as in all the men who are pictured to us in the Old Testament as leaders of the nation in spiritual matters, two elements met and blended; the first was the influence of the past, in the form of national characteristics and customs whose tendency was in the direction of the

heathenism and barbarism seen among other nations, and in the lives of a large element in Israel; the second was the divine impulse, the spiritual illumination, which became dominant in their lives in the degree that it was able to remove the limitations of character already present. The result varied with the man, but in every case the true prophet occupied a position above his fellows, and was capable of teaching them higher truths concerning God and righteousness.

2. Moses was the leader under whom Israel emerged from the tribal or clan period, and entered upon the consciousness of nationality. Like later prophets, he was raised up of God at a crisis in the life of his people. The experiences of Israel in Egypt had prepared them in some measure for an independent career, and Moses himself had passed through such discipline as fitted him to become a leader. Reared in the court of Egypt, with all the educational advantages belonging to a prince of the blood, his first attempt to emancipate his brethren was premature (Ex. 2:11-15; Acts 7:25), and he was forced to find safety in flight. Forty years were spent in Midian, which were no less years of preparation; and at last the call of God came to him, and he was sent to effect the release of his people from Egyptian servitude (Ex. 3). This purpose was accomplished by him, acting under divine direction, in spite of the skepticism of the people themselves and the determined

opposition of the King of Egypt. The Exodus was attended with such signs of divine power in the discomfiture of Egypt and the safeguarding of Israel, that it was long regarded as the most signal proof of Jehovah's power and providential purpose for the chosen nation. Moses' leadership continued through another forty years, during which the people received the law at Mount Sinai, and accomplished that period of probation and discipline in the wilderness which fitted them in some measure for the arduous enterprises ahead. Moses laid down his leadership only when Israel had at last reached the borders of Canaan and was ready for its career of conquest.

3. Moses is usually considered a law-giver rather than a prophet; but it is as a prophet that he must be regarded primarily. This is the title given him more than once in the Old Testament (Deut. 34:10; Hos. 12:13), and all his other functions of law-giver, judge and statesman grew out of his prophetic character. He gave Israel its being as a nation, developing a body of slaves into a great and independent people. He organized a form of worship with a movable sanctuary, at which the regular forms of service were to be observed; he delivered to Israel a body of institutes grouped about the Decalogue or "Ten Words," which served as the national constitution throughout the subsequent history. These laws (which appear in their most primitive form in Ex. 20—23, 34) are not merely rubrics for

ceremonial observances, nor minute regulations of conduct; they are rather illustrations of the principles of mercy, justice and humanity, and though in comparison with the teaching of Jesus they were very imperfect, still if contrasted with the prevailing ideas of Moses's day they are seen to be just, merciful and elevating. In addition, Moses set apart a body of men to act as priests, selecting them from his own tribe, and placing at their head his brother Aaron. To these men were committed the duties of ministering at the sanctuary and of acting as the religious teachers of the nation, especially in matters relating to the law, though others, such as kings, prophets and common people had also the right to sacrifice (Jud. 6:24-26; 13:19; 1 Sam. 14:34, 35; 2 Sam. 6:17, 18). Thus the general features of Israel's organization by Moses did not differ externally from those to be found among other nations of that age. Such elements as sacrifice, feasts, sacred seasons, circumcision, sanctuary and priesthood were in use elsewhere; indeed, there is hardly a feature of the external side of Israel's civil or religious life which does not find a parallel in the customs of neighboring and older nations. It is not in these elements that the uniqueness and originality of the Hebrew faith consist, but in the new truths which were revealed and which were now enforced by customs which in other nations had far other meanings. Among these ideas revealed to Israel are found the unity and personality of God (Ex. 15:13), who is both righteous and holy, who in Moses' day began to be known to Israel by the covenant name Jahveh, or Jehovah (Ex. 3:14, 15; 6:2-4); the sinfulness of idolatry; and the necessity that the people should partake of the ethical character of their God. The standard of morality and worship was high for the age. Indeed, it was the first serious attempt to unite morality with religion. In these regards the system which Moses left to Israel was in striking contrast with the religions of other nations, which were so largely characterized by speculation, superstition, polytheism, cruelty, and sensuality. Moses, therefore, stands as the most majestic figure in the early life of the nation; a figure so important and lofty that his influence is plainly traced throughout all the subsequent history as the great prophet and spiritual leader, the organizer of Israel's national life.

4. Among the promises made by Moses for the future was one to the effect that the nation should not be left without spiritual oversight and direction, but should be given from time to time a prophet, who should speak in behalf of God (Deut. 18:15-22). This promise clearly implies that the priesthood was not sufficient to accomplish the purposes of spiritual leadership. Nevertheless, it was many years after the death of Moses before another prophet arose who was worthy to be compared with him. Israel entered and conquered Canaan, and when Joshua had passed away a succession of

judges ruled in various parts of the land, among whom was Deborah, who is called a prophetess (Jud. 4). But it was not until Samuel appeared that the prophetic function was revived, as it had been exercised by Moses. Under this new leader the people passed from the anarchy and confusion of the judges to the organization and order of the days of David. Samuel was of the tribe of Ephraim (1 Sam. 1:1), but he was early taken into the tabernacle service, and ministered often in priestly offices. After the death of Eli, the priest in office, Samuel undertook the leadership of Israel, and for a score of years worked silently toward the realization of national ideas. Little appreciated at first, and looked upon as a mere clairvoyant or fortune-teller, whose advice might be sought by those in trouble (1 Sam. 9:6-9), he came at length to be regarded as the real national leader. Perhaps the sincerest compliment ever paid him was the popular demand for a king, which, in spite of its seeming disregard of his leadership over the people, indicated the sense of unity, solidarity and national pride fostered by him, so foreign to the days of the judges. A king was chosen in the person of Saul, son of Kish, but he was not equal to the emergency. He was unable or unwilling to see that obedience to the divine will was the secret of power (1 Sam. 15:22), and his rejection was the result. Meantime, Samuel was pursuing his task of building up a new national life. His method was not political

The Beginnings of Prophecy 33

revolution, but religious reformation. From his home in Ramah he went on visits, almost pastoral in character, to places of ancestral sacredness like Gilgal, Mizpeh, Bethlehem and Bethel, where sacrificial feasts were held, and the sanctions of the true faith laid upon the hearts of the people (1 Sam. 7:5, 9; 10:8; 16:4, 5).

5. In connection with the work of Samuel, we first learn of the "sons of the prophets." These were bodies of men devoted to the national religion, but closely resembling the similar orders in the service of Baal of whom we catch a glimpse at a later time (1 Kings 17:29). In Israel the bands of prophets in the early days of Samuel were of this character, made up of enthusiasts who went about the country rousing themselves to a high pitch of ecstasy by means of music, and no doubt preaching the religion of Jehovah in the fierce spirit of the age. In the circle of such "prophesying" the bystander might be seized with the same enthusiasm, utter similar words, and fall unconscious on the ground. These manifestations were believed to be divinely induced (1 Sam. 10:5-13; 19:18-24). Nothing speaks more eloquently for the wisdom of Samuel than the fact that with all his lofty purpose he did not despise the good these bands of men could accomplish. Crude as their methods might be, he even identified himself with them in a measure, and by assuming their leadership (1 Sam. 19:20), he gradually made of them organizations effective in the propagation of

the saner and loftier conceptions of Jehovah and His religion, which appeared in his own work and that of his successors. These bands seem to have been localized and trained by Samuel and were made capable of spreading his instruction among the people. In the days of Elijah and Elisha the schools of the prophets were already an important factor in the religious life of the nation. There was an element of fierce zeal in Samuel's character, but he lived in one of the most critical periods of the history, when righteousness needed to be emphasized in no uncertain way. No loftier prophetic note was ever struck than that uttered by this man of God in the famous words, "To obey is better than sacrifice and to hearken than the fat of rams" (1 Sam. 15:22).

REFERENCES

I. The life of Abraham, Gen. 11: 26; 25: 11.
II. The career of Moses.
1. His early life, Ex. 2: 1-10. 2. His life in Midian, Ex. 2: 11—4: 26. 3. At the court of Egypt, Ex. 4: 27—12: 36. 4. The exodus and the journey, Ex. 12: 37—19: 25; Num. 33: 1-49. 5. Death of Moses, Deut. 34: 1-12.
III. The work of Samuel.
1. His early life and relation to Eli, 1 Sam. 1-4. 2. His ministry as judge and reformer, 1 Sam. 7-25.

QUESTIONS

1. With what did Israel's selection begin? When did the national life have its starting point? What may be said of the character of Abraham? What other patriarchs had an important part in the history? What two elements entered into the making of these

The Beginnings of Prophecy 35

and other religious leaders of Israel? What was the prophet's relation to the people? 2. What was the special work of Moses? How was he prepared for his mission? Against what obstacles did he have to contend? How does the exodus stand related to the national life? Of what was it the proof? What were some of the later events of Moses' career? 3. What was Moses' great work? What was the place of the law of Moses in Israel's history? What is the character of this law? Whom did he appoint as religious leaders and teachers? Wherein lay the significance of Israel's institutes and religious services? What religious ideas were emphasized by Moses? How did they differ from the ideas of other nations? What is Moses' true place in history? 4. What was the promise left by Moses regarding a line of prophets? Who was the first great prophet after Moses? What did he do? What was the result of his reforms? At what places did he hold sacrificial services? 5. Who were the "sons of the prophets"? What was the character of their work? How did Samuel use them? What later prophets were closely associated with the prophetic guilds? What was Samuel's disposition? What is one of his great sayings?

CHAPTER IV

ELIJAH AND ELISHA

1. The reign of David (c. 1017-977 B. C.) gives evidence of the lasting impress of Samuel's work; indeed, the reforms of the great prophet had made possible such a kingdom. David was himself a man of deeply religious nature, to which witness is borne by his interest in righteousness both in his individual subjects and in the nation as a whole. The blemishes upon his character are many, but they were the faults of the age in which he lived, and he must be judged by its standards, not by those of our own day. His spirit of penitence after his great sin is most impressive as contrasted with the godless conduct of monarchs generally in those centuries. He brought up the ark which had lain in obscurity during the reign of Saul, and established it in Jerusalem (2 Sam. 6), which was thus made not only the political but the religious center of the kingdom. But the most important contribution which David made to Israel's spiritual life was the psalm material which he left, and which became the model of a great body of devotional utterances in later years. Just how many or what psalms David composed may not be certain, but some of those most precious to the Church in all ages since are believed to have come from him

(*e. g.*, 19, 8, 24, 15, 32, 51, 23, etc.), and such expressions of faith, confidence in God, contrition for sin, and certainty of its disastrous consequences are sufficient to entitle David to the place among the prophets which Peter assigned him (Acts 2:29, 30). Yet the deference which he ever paid to Nathan, the prophet of his court, shows that he regarded him as his superior, and recognized the fact that the normal position of a prophet of God was above that of king. Nathan seems to have been a counsellor of the king's (2 Sam. 7:1-17; 12:1-15; 1 Kings 1), and to have written an account of his reign (1 Chr. 29:29). There is no evidence that he pursued a public ministry of teaching and preaching like that of Samuel. Another prophet appears in connection with David's life, Gad, who was both adviser and biographer of his royal friend (1 Sam. 22:5; 2 Sam. 24:11; 1 Chr. 29:29).

2. The reign of Solomon was a time when prophecy enjoyed less freedom than in the past. The position of the various elements in national leadership was reversed. In David's time the prophet was first in importance, and next to him the king, with the priesthood following. In Solomon's reign the king was first, with the priests in the next position, and the prophets below them in favor. Perhaps this was owing to the absence of any strong prophets; but it was probably due quite as much to the secular tendency of Solomon's nature. The temple itself, though a magnificent structure, had

the effect of heightening the beauty and impressiveness of Jerusalem as the royal capital rather than of deepening the religious life of the nation. The prophets apparently regarded with apprehension the royal policy of alliances with foreign courts, which, though it increased the wealth of the nation, broke down those safeguards by which Israel had been sheltered from contact with the heathen world. The success or failure of the national faith depended on its having opportunity to develop without contamination from without. The policy of Solomon made such seclusion impossible. It is not surprising therefore that the greatest of the prophets of this reign, Ahijah of Shiloh, promoted, if he did not first suggest, the revolt of the ten tribes under Jeroboam (1 Kings 11:26-40). From the effects of this separation into two kingdoms the nation never recovered. Henceforth it was impossible for Israel ever to be a great world-state, and thus the religious idea which was the foundation of its life had greater opportunity to expand, and the division of the kingdom is seen to have been in accordance with the divine purpose (1 Kings 12:15). Unfortunately Jeroboam failed to realize the hopes which the prophets reposed in him. His reverence for them gave way before his fears regarding the perpetuity of his kingdom, and he accordingly sought to strengthen himself by devices which essentially corrupted the worship of the north, such as the erection of two golden bulls as images of Jehovah, the change of the times of the feasts and the elevation of common people to the priesthood (1 Kings 12:26-33). For these acts of treachery to the power by which he was elevated he was always held in disfavor by the prophets to the end of the history, and regarded as having set the example of disobedience followed so faithfully by the kings of Israel (1 Kings 14:1-20; 15:26, 30, 34; 16:19, 26, 31).

3. The reign of Ahab of Israel (875-853 B. C.) brought to an open issue the question which had divided the prophets from the kings in the days of Solomon and Jeroboam. Two theories of the state confronted each other in the persons of Ahab and Elijah. The latter was the advocate of national seclusion. All that tended to bring the people into contact with other nations, whether war or commerce, met with his stern disapproval. To kings like Ahab this seemed a narrow policy. National prosperity, so it seemed to him, was to be obtained only through friendly relations with other states, and to this end alliances by marriage were sought with foreign courts. Ahab accordingly entered into treaty relations with Ethbaal, king of Zidon, and married his daughter, Jezebel, giving her religion, viz., the worship of Baal and Astarte, official sanction in his capital, Samaria, by the side of the religion of Jehovah (1 Kings 16:29-33). While it is improbable that Ahab renounced entirely the faith of his nation, yet the worshipers, and especially the prophets, of Jehovah were

subjected to ill-treatment and persecution
(1 Kings 18:3, 4). Under the favor of the
court the foreign cult made rapid progress
until it appeared that the whole nation had
been swept away by the seductive Phœnician
worship (1 Kings 19:14). But the counter
movement came. Its center was in the
prophetic circle, and its leader was Elijah.
His first effort at reformátion (1 Kings
18: 1-41) was only partially successful
(1 Kings, 19:1-3), and he learned that abrupt
and bloody methods are not always wisest
(1 Kings 19: 11, 12). In the experience of
Elijah at the mount lay the profoundest
lesson for the prophets to ponder. The
power of God was manifested not so much in
the spectacular forms of activity as in the
silent ones. It was the voice, the message
that was needed, not the sword. This was
the keynote of all later prophecy; it was a
message, an utterance from God in the lives
and through the lips of His servants.

4. Elijah perceived that new rulers were
needed both in Israel and Syria, and predicted their advent (1 Kings 19:15, 16).
When Ahab transgressed the limits of his
rights and trespassed on those of a citizen,
the prophet spoke like a fearless tribune of
the people in denunciation of the act (1
Kings 21:17-22). He represents the rugged,
inflexible champion of God, like Samuel;
and he possessed the same fierce zeal which
characterized that prophet. His relation to
the sons of the prophets was similar to that
sustained by the earlier leader, though the

character of these bands appears to have changed materially since Samuel's day. They dwelt in communities, as at Bethel and Jericho (2 Kings 2:3, 5), in houses which they erected (2 Kings 6:1). They looked upon Elijah as their leader, and had intimation of his approaching departure (2 Kings 2:1f.). Perhaps they were also distinguished, like Elijah, by their garments (2 Kings 1:8), as they seem to have been by their tonsured heads (1 Kings 20:41; 2 Kings 2:23). They at times resorted to curious devices to enforce their messages (1 Kings 20:35-43); they were probably regarded by the people generally with some measure of respect, though hardly by the soldiers (2 Kings 9:1, 11), who perhaps saw only the grotesque features of the order. Even Elisha employed a minstrel on one occasion to induce the requisite ecstasy (2 Kings 3:15). But the character of Elijah is most impressive. With the boldness of a hero he proclaimed the true faith in a time of gravest peril, and well earned the right to be regarded, along with Moses, as among the greatest prophets of the Old Testament, not unworthy to stand with the Christ on the Mount of Transfiguration. He was a greater safeguard to the state than armies, and Elisha well characterized his master when, as he saw him ascending heavenward, he cried, "My father, my father, the chariots of Israel and the horsemen thereof" (2 Kings 2:12).

5. It was but natural that Elisha should be his successor. He was in striking con-

trast to him in all respects. Elijah was the earthquake; Elisha was the still small voice. His presence was a benediction. He was a pastor, a shepherd to his people. Elijah called him in that mysterious, enigmatical manner peculiar to him (1 Kings 19:19-21), and from that day he continued with him. The relation between the two men was intimate, though their natures were so different. Elisha's request at the moment of his master's departure was that a double portion of that spirit which had been the prophetic guide of Israel for years might rest upon him (2 Kings 2:9). Like Elijah, he wrought miracles, not merely of power, but of beneficence. His fame went abroad into other lands, and Naaman, the captain of the king of Syria, came to Samaria to have Elisha heal him of his leprosy. Around the character of this remarkable man are woven some of the most interesting of Old Testament narratives; and his life so impressed the nation that when he died in the reign of Joash, the king came to his house and voiced his sense of the loss which he and the kingdom sustained, in the historic words already used by the prophet regarding his master, "My father, my father, the chariots of Israel and the horsemen thereof (2 Kings 13:15).

REFERENCES

I. The life of David, 1 Sam. 16: 1—1 Kings 2.
II. The career of Elijah, 1 Kings 17:19, 21; 2 Kings 1: 2.
III. The work of Elisha, 2 Kings 2: 6, 8, 9, 13.

QUESTIONS

1. In what respect may David be counted among the prophets? How does he compare with other kings of the period? What contribution does the psalm material make to the study of religion in Israel? What relation did Nathan sustain to David and the kingdom? What other prophet is named in connection with this period? 2. What was the condition of prophecy during the reign of Solomon? What relation did it sustain to the kingship and priesthood? How did the prophets look upon the royal policy of expansion? What was their idea as to the best policy to be pursued? Who assisted or encouraged Jeroboam in his revolt? How did Jeroboam disappoint the prophets? 3. What was the character of Ahab from the standpoint of secular affairs? What was Ahab's course in increasing the prosperity of the kingdom? What was the result to the Hebrew religion? Who headed the movement for reform? What lesson did Elijah learn? 4. What was the character of Elijah? What was his relation to the sons of the prophets, and what was their character? How does Elijah rank with the other prophets of the Old Testament? 5. In what respect was Elisha a contrast to Elijah? What miracles were wrought by these prophets? How did Elisha's reputation extend beyond Israel? How was Elisha regarded by the king and people of Israel?

CHAPTER V

AMOS, THE PROPHET OF RIGHTEOUSNESS

1. It was the reign of Jeroboam II. (781-740 B. C.) that witnessed the period of greatest importance for religion in the northern kingdom. During these years the work of Amos was accomplished, and that of Hosea begun. These were the first prophets whose preaching has been preserved for us. This new phase of prophecy may almost be called a new beginning, for here we are able for the first time to study the materials that reveal the true condition of the kingdom, and exhibit the new tone of the prophetic work. Amos and Hosea were not, however, a new order of men. They recognized the fact that they were continuing the labors of prophets before them (Amos 2:11; 3:7), but the tone of the prophetic ministry is higher and the vision of the divine nature and purpose wider and clearer. Jeroboam ranked with Ahab as a successful monarch. His kingdom was greatly extended, surpassing in extent even the territory of Solomon, for he conquered many of the districts lost in the reign of his immediate predecessors, and to these he added Damascus and even distant Hamath (2 Kings 14:23-29). The prophet Jonah appears to have lived in his reign, and was, perhaps, an adviser of the king's (2 Kings 14:25). The kingdom was

in prosperous condition, and the dangers which such prosperity brings were plainly seen by Amos. There was a growing separation between the rich and the poor, and the sins that grow out of such a condition are set down (Amos 2:6-8; 3:12, 15; 5:7, 10, 11; 6:4-6). The popular religion was of a low and formal character, and it is difficult at times to be sure whether the description is that of the degraded Jehovah worship which resulted from the erection of the images by Jeroboam, or of the heathen customs that crept in (Amos 2:12; 4:4f.; 5:21; 8:5). In such an age it was necessary that a strong voice be lifted in protest against the spirit of the times and in defense of righteousness. Amos was that voice.

2. His home was in Tekoah, a small town in the kingdom of Judah, and his work included the duties of a herdsman and a dresser of sycamore trees (Amos 1:1; 7:14). It was not, however, to the people of Judah that he was sent, but to those of the northern country. Like that other prophet who in the days of Jeroboam I. came from the south to Bethel to speak a message against its altar (1 Kings 13:1f.), so Amos suddenly appeared in that city consecrated to the bull-image of Jehovah, and uttered his message of stern reproof. He was not a member of the prophetic order, those men who performed the duties of religious teachers, the successors of the "sons of the prophets" in the times of Samuel and Elijah. Indeed, these men seem to have become in this

period little more than professional proclaimers of traditional ideas, with no true message from God, but practicing their trade as a means of livelihood. To be even classed with such men Amos regarded as an insult, and repudiated any relations with them (Amos 7:14). In his business of merchant in cattle and fruit he had perhaps been able to observe the conditions prevailing in the cities of both Judah and Israel, and with a soul impressed with the divine character through the teachings of earlier prophets, he was selected to bear to Bethel the word of God for his generation. In what form the prophetic call came to him we are not informed, but he intimates that necessity was laid upon him to undertake his difficult task (Amos 3:8; 7:15). The length of his stay in Bethel is not recorded, but after a time his plain, fearless preaching, perhaps uttered in the market-place thronged by men of his class, came to the attention of Amaziah, the leading priest of the popular cult, who reported to the king the conduct of this Judean peasant who was denouncing the government and the religion of Israel (Amos 7:10, 11). He also warned Amos to return to Judah and there ply his prophetic trade if he would, but to cease giving offense to the court and the ecclesiastics at that ancient city. Then the prophet turned upon him with indignation, disclaiming any professional or mercenary motive, and forewarning him of the fate that should overtake his own family and the entire nation (Amos 7:14-17). Beyond these few facts, nothing is known of Amos. He probably returned soon after to his home, and committed to writing the substance of his preaching at Bethel, which is happily thus preserved to us.

3. The first section of the book, which may indeed be the first of his sermons, is highly artistic in form, and rises to a climax of rare power (chapters 1, 2). After the introductory note referring to the time at which Amos preached (1:1), and the statement of his usual theme or text (1:2), there is given the arraignment of the nations by which Israel was surrounded. Like many other prophetic utterances of similar character, these threats of punishment for sin are really addressed to Israel as impressing the consequences of wrong-doing, although they appear to be intended as messages to the various nations named. Amos speaks of Damascus, Gaza, Tyre, Edom, Ammon, Moab and Judah as the ones who shall suffer for their transgressions. In each of these seven cases one particular sin is mentioned, with the implication that others might be named. All save Judah are held accountable to the common duties of humanity, and are reproved for barbarity and forewarned of their chastisement. But Judah is judged by the higher law of God's revelation, which imposes greater responsibilities. Then, having drawn the line of judgment about Israel by this roll-call of impending wrath, he touches the heart of his theme, the sins of Israel, and the retribution which must follow

(2:6f.). Here again he insists upon the higher standard of conduct. The nation is not examined regarding such sins as those for which the heathen nations were condemned. It is taken for granted that God's people are above such grossness and barbarism. But judged by the ethical standards of the prophets their conduct is sufficiently black. They oppress the poor and betray the cause of the innocent for paltry bribes; they lead their children in ways of impurity and use their positions of honor or trust to minister to their own pleasures; and all this after a singularly impressive history in which God had been showing Himself their protector. Even He was weary of such conduct on their part. The end could only be destruction.

4. Amos saw clearly the responsibility which arose out of divine selection for service, and that of one to whom much had been given, much would be required. Therefore, he startled the men of Israel, who were trusting for safety to the fact that they were the chosen of God, with the words, "You only have I known of all the families of the earth, therefore I will visit upon you all your iniquities" (3:2). The course of indulgence and oppression now being pursued was an astonishment even to other nations (3:9; 6:1-8), and could only result in disaster. Especially were the women rebuked (4:1-3), for the prophet saw that to their ostentatious vanity much of the commercial fraud and judicial dishonesty of their husbands was

due; and he knew that the moral condition of a people never rises above the level of its womanhood. Disasters had already come in the form of famine, drought, blight, locusts and war (4:6-11), but had been of no avail. A heavier judgment must now be announced. The real difficulty back of all, however, was the failure to understand the power and greatness of God. The worship at the shrines of Bethel and Dan had tended to degrade the popular idea of Jehovah to the level of the gods of the nations. Indeed, it was at all times difficult for the Israelite to conceive of God as absolute and supreme. To him it was more natural to accept the generally prevalent idea that each tribe or nation had its own god, who was to be worshiped by his people within his own territory; but outside this limit one came under the jurisdiction of other gods which were recognized by Israel as having as real an existence as Jehovah. Thus the popular Hebrew thought of Jehovah was rather monolatry than monotheism. It was only the great prophets who understood and sought to impress the truth. Amos was of this number. Nothing can exceed the power and beauty of his words on this theme (5:8). Moreover, Jehovah is a righteous God, and demands righteousness on the part of His worshipers. He cares nothing for the ritual of feasts and solemn assemblies, burnt offerings and sacrifices (5:21-23). All these acts may have a value as aids to devotion, but they can never be made a substitute for it.

What is needed is right conduct (v. 24). In these utterances Amos strikes the keynote of his entire message.

5. The section 7:1—9:10 is devoted to a series of visions in which the prophet received fresh light upon the national prospects, and whose relation served the purpose of religious instruction. They present the impending judgments of God upon His unfaithful people under various pictures of disaster. Now a plague of locusts is predicted, and withheld at the prophet's intercession (7:1-3). A similar prayer turns aside a devastating conflagration (vs. 4-6). Once more, a measuring line, often the symbol of destruction, is seen in the Lord's hand, and the seer is assured that there shall be no more delay (vs. 7-9). At this point the visions are interrupted by the episode of Amos's interview with the priest Amaziah, to which reference has already been made (vs. 10-17). Then follows the vision of the basket of over-ripe summer fruit, a symbol of the nation, and the denunciation of woes to come in consequence of dishonest dealings and injustice (8:1-14). The series closes with the vision of the shattered temple and the terrified worshipers, who shall be unable to escape (9:1-10). The book comes to its end with a message, in striking contrast with its other utterances, in which are included the promise of restoration to the house of David after the approaching destruction has passed by, and the prosperity that may then be expected (9:11-15). Amos

Amos, the Prophet of Righteousness 51

stood alone, a solitary witness for God among a strange people hostile to him. But he was a fearless champion of the truth, a faithful proclaimer of the righteousness of God.

THE BOOK OF AMOS

I. The prologue; sin brings punishment, chaps. 1, 2.
   1. The title and date, 1: 1. 2. The text of the prophecy, 1: 2. 3. Israel's neighbors, Damascus, Gaza, Tyre, Edom, Ammon, Moab, and even Judah, shall be punished for their sins, 1:3—2: 5. 4. Israel, having sinned (6: 8) in spite of warning (9) and blessings (10, 11), and having corrupted or silenced religious teachers (12), shall also suffer (13-16).

II. The condemnation of Israel, 3—6.
   1. First section; Israel from the world's standpoint, 3: 1-15. 2. Second section; Israel's sins and warnings, 4: 1-13. 3. Third section; Israel and God, 5: 1-17. 4. Fourth section; Israel's worthless ritual, 5: 18-27. 5. Fifth section; Israel's worthless rulers, 6: 1-14.

III. A series of visions, 7: 1—9: 10.
   1. The locusts; the prophet's plea, 7: 1-3. 2. The fire; the prophet's plea, 4: 6. 3. The plumb line; no more immunity, 7-9 [An episode (10-17); false charge of the priest of Bethel against Amos (10, 11); the prophet commanded to leave (12, 13); his indignant reply (14-17).] 4. Basket of summer fruit, 8: 1-14. 5. Shattered temple and scattered worshipers, 9: 1-10.

IV. The epilogue; words of hope, 9: 11-15.
   1. David's house is to be restored, 11, 12. 2. Great prosperity, 13. 3. Scattered Israel to be restored to their land forever, 14, 15.

QUESTIONS

1. In whose reign did Amos and Hosea appear? In what respect did their work differ from that of the former prophets? What was the character of Jeroboam's reign? What were the social, political and

religious conditions prevalent in that period? 2. Where was Amos' home and what was his business? To what city did he come to preach? What relation did he bear to the prophets of the times? Why was he selected to be a prophet? Who was angered by his words? How did Amos reply to his rebuke? 3. What was the text of Amos' preaching? What nations did he denounce for sin? To what standard were Judah and Israel held accountable? What sins in Israel does Amos rebuke? 4. What obligations did Amos associate with Israel's selection? Why were the women rebuked? What was the influence of the popular worship? What was the popular thought regarding God? What is Amos' teaching on this subject? 5. Give an outline of the visions of Amos. What was the nature of the interview between Amaziah and Amos? What is the hope expressed regarding the restoration of the house of David?

CHAPTER VI

HOSEA, THE PROPHET OF DIVINE LOVE

1. Unlike Amos, who left his own country to bear the message of God to another people, Hosea was a native of the kingdom of Israel, and he spoke out of a heart full not only of devotion to the divine will, but of affection for his land. His call to the prophetic office grew out of different causes from those which operated in the selection of Amos. It was the character and disposition of the latter that made him a fitting messenger of God. But Hosea had passed through an experience of domestic trouble which opened his eyes to the long-suffering love of God toward a sinful people, and prepared him to be the bearer of his message. His ministry lies in the period immediately following that of Amos, whom he may have heard in Bethel. But it was a longer ministry than that of the Judean prophet, covering not only the closing portion of the prosperous reign of Jeroboam II., to which chapters 1-3 probably belong, but extending into the chaotic years of Israel's decline and fall, which came on so swiftly. Jeroboam was succeeded by his son Zechariah, who was slain after six months. Then came Shallum with a reign of only a month, ending in assassination. Menahem, his slayer,

reigned a few years (740-737 B. C.) by purchasing the favor of Assyria (2 Kings 15:17-20), leaving the kingdom to his son Pekahiah, who after two years was murdered by Pekah, his captain. The latter ascended the tottering throne, but suffered the same fate at the hands of Hoshea, the last king of Israel, whose capital, Samaria, was taken by Sargon, king of Assyria, in 721 B. C. Thus ended the history of the northern kingdom. How long the prophet Hosea's life extended into this troubled period we have no means of determining, but many of its characteristic features are reflected in the second portion of his book (chapters 4-14). In the writings of Amos, as has been seen, there is given a lifelike picture of the political, social and religious conditions of the reign of Jeroboam. Similarly in Hosea are presented the features of the dark days into which the nation immediately plunged. It was a time of conspiracies and assassinations, which followed each other in such rapid succession that one deed of blood seemed to touch another (Hos. 4:2; 8:4; 10:7). In consequence, the kingdom was distracted and the princes were conspicuous examples of depravity, leading their kings into dissipation only to end by murdering them (Hos. 7:1f.). There was no definite political policy; some wanted to form alliance with Assyria, others advocated Egypt as helper (Hos. 5:13; 7:11; 8:9). Meantime, general demoralization and corruption prevailed (Hos. 4:18; 5:10; 6:9; 9:9). It was not easy to discharge the duties of a prophet in such a time; yet such was the task committed to Hosea.

2. The first three chapters of the book are descriptive of the prophet's preparation for his work. This was wrought by a tragedy in his domestic experience whose effect changed the whole current of his life. He married Gomer, a woman whom he sincerely loved, but who proved unfaithful to him. Three children were born in the household, to whom were given names significant of coming events—retribution upon the house of Jehu and the rejection of Israel—but also partially expressive of the father's distress and doubt. Presently Gomer deserted her husband, or was banished from his house as no longer worthy to abide there. But his love for her was not quenched, and sitting in his desolate house he could not fail to perceive the analogy between his bereaved estate and that of Jehovah, who had chosen Israel as he, the prophet, had married Gomer, but who had been more than once abandoned by the unfaithful nation for lovers powerless to help, viz., the other gods in whose worship the people were continually going astray. Hosea saw that idolatry was not only a sin against the divine law, but an insult to the divine love. And yet in spite of all, God still loved Israel and was willing to welcome back the nation in spite of all its sin. Out of this bitter experience Hosea brought his message. It was of a character to be spoken only by one who had suffered, and who could thereby enter into

the problem of God's long-suffering love for the sinful. The divine Spirit could use Hosea as no other man of his generation was capable of being used, and though the experience was one through which many another Israelite may have passed in that time of seductive and idolatrous practices, still Hosea saw that his unhappy lot was a providential preparation for a ministry to which he now devoted his full strength. It is with this retrospective and illuminated vision of those agonies of the past through which he had come that he writes the narrative. But there was still another step to be taken. His own sorrow and love had taught him to understand the love of God. This was now the message he was prepared to bring to Israel. But it came to its complete expression in his own life when he went forth, conquering pride and all sense of injury done him, and found the woman who had once been his wife, bought her from the slavery into which she had fallen, and restored her to the calm and the love of his home, where he hoped that in time she might grow, under the discipline of love and patience, to be worthy once more of the name of wife. Thus the prophet's message from God to Israel, a message suited not only to that age, but to every age, because first of all incarnated in Hosea's own life.

3. The condition of the kingdom was sufficiently alarming to disquiet the most hopeful. If the common people were going astray, it was because their leaders set the

example. This was true of priests and prophets as well as princes. One of the greatest obstacles to the work of the true prophets was the activity of the professional religious teachers of the time, who pursued courses which gave the people an utterly false idea of their moral and spiritual obligations. Hosea complains that the people are destroyed because of lack of knowledge (4:6), and that the priests are actually eager to increase transgression in order to multiply the offerings; and thus they feed on sin (v. 8). Still worse, the prophet accuses the priests of murder, highway robbery and foulness of life (6:9). Such conduct on the part of the recognized authorities in religious matters either brought all worship into contempt, or quieted the consciences of the people regarding their own lives, and thus rendered doubly difficult the work of a true prophet, who was thought to be a madman (9:7), or was beset with plots and snares, as may have been Hosea's experience (9:8). The civil rulers are not behind the priests in wickedness. They are dishonest (5:10). But far worse than this, they deliberately debauch their kings, and then murder them to accomplish their selfish ends (7:3-7; 10:7; 13:10). As a consequence, there is no stability of government. Ephraim (the prophet's usual name for the kingdom of Israel, taken from its strongest tribe) attempts to support his waning power by alliances with other people (7:11). "He mixeth himself among the nations" (7:8), but he has no safe political plans. He is "a cake not turned," half baked. The signs of premature old age are upon him (7:9); in his inability to meet the present crisis and through it enter upon a larger life, he is like a child that dies upon the threshold of birth (13:13). The effect of such conditions upon the popular life was deplorable. The people were like their priests (4:9). The most debasing practices gained rapid way among them, so that domestic purity was well-nigh impossible (4:11-14; 9:9). Wealth was gained at the expense of honesty (12:7). Idolatry, which the prophet calls characteristically adultery or whoredom, prevails on every side. The result can only be national ruin. The Assyrian, already on the horizon, shall be their destruction (8:14; 10:5, 6, 14, 15; 11:5), and they shall go into exile in Egypt (9:6). Thus we are enabled to see the exact character of public and private life in Israel through the eyes of the prophet. His was not a message of wrath, but of tender love. Yet he was compelled to announce to the nation the certain results of its misdeeds. God is too merciful ever to divorce sin from its consequences.

4. This mingling of denunciation with loving entreaty gives to Hosea a vibrancy of tone nowhere else found among the prophets. As in former days he had watched with loving solicitude every sign of repentance and reformation on the part of his erring wife, only to be plunged again and again into torments of jealous anger by her waywardness

and relapses into sin; so with the same anxiety he, as the representative of God, marks every token of penitence shown by the people; rejoicing in their occasional promises of better things, only to find that their reformation is transient and ineffectual. In such moments of painful discovery he breaks forth in a very passion of righteous fury, as jealous for God as he might have been for himself. At such moments he is a very personification of divine wrath. "I am unto them as a lion; as a leopard will I watch by the way: I will meet them like a bear that is bereaved of her whelps, and will rend the caul of their heart. It is thy destruction, O Israel, that thou art against me, against thy help" (13:7-9). He warns Judah against association with Israel, and a consequent share in its ruin. "Though Israel play the harlot, let not Judah offend" (4:15); "Ephraim is joined to his idols; let him alone," lest you too fall under a similar chastisement (v. 17). Yet Hosea can never quite believe that Israel is past redemption, and continually pleads with the nation to return to God (6:13); and though fresh evidences of sin astonish and grieve the prophet till he cries out like a distressed mother over a wayward son (6:4), and even once comes to the conclusion that all is lost, and invokes death and the grave to come and do their worst with such a hopeless race of sinners, vowing that now at last he will not again change his purpose (13:14), yet even this seemingly irrevocable doom is suspended, and the prophet returns to his former yearning mood (11:8, 9), closing his book with a beautiful colloquy, in which he once more extends the divine invitation, which now the nation seemingly accepts, pledging faithfulness to Jehovah for the future (14:1-9).

5. Thus both Amos and Hosea reveal the growing power of prophecy as the disclosure of the divine will through men specially chosen and prepared to give it utterance. The one speaks a message of warning and judgment; the other of the love and mercy of God. To both Israel is the chosen nation; but this is not the ground of pride, rather of responsibility. Monotheism is distinctly recognized; heathen nations are under the government of Jehovah. Especially is there noticeable an advance in prophetic ideals, a larger interpretation of the divine will than in former times. Amos holds even a heathen nation accountable for barbarities which in former times David committed with apparently no apprehension that he was transgressing the ordinary customs of his age (2 Sam. 12:29-31; cf. Amos 1:3). Similarly Hosea pronounces punishment upon the house of Jehu for his bloody conduct at Jezreel, which had met the full approbation of the prophets of that period (2 Kings 9:7; 10:30; cf. Hos. 4:1). The prophets were not perfect men, nor were their messages final. They spoke and wrought as they were moved by the divine Spirit, but the Spirit had to use them as they were, with their

Hosea, the Prophet of Divine Love 61

limitations of view and their hereditary instincts. It is not strange, therefore, that each new generation of prophets was able to take higher ground and bring to the nation a more adequate knowledge of God. The doctrine of divine love preached by Hosea marked an advance over any previous prophetic message. Such ideals were found nowhere save in this chosen nation. Natural development will not produce an Amos or a Hosea, much less an Isaiah. The divine purpose and the divine Spirit afford the only explanation. Slowly disclosed in the lives of men as they were prepared to understand and embody it, the centuries witnessed among the Hebrew people the most remarkable manifestation of moral and spiritual development which history records, a development whose end was not the elevation of one nation alone, but of all the world.

THE BOOK OF HOSEA

I. Hosea's domestic tragedy and its lessons, 1-3.
   1. His wife and children, 1: 2-9. Gomer, Jezreel (valley of bloodshed), Lo-ruhamah (unpitied), Lo-ammi (not my people). 2. The nation's unfaithfulness and return to God, 2: 2-23. 3. Restoration and discipline of Hosea's wife, 3.
II. Sermons regarding Israel's sin and God's love, 4-14.
   1. The people encouraged to sin by wicked leaders, 4. 2. Accusations and impending wrath, 5,6. 3. The penalty of rejected help, 7: 1—9: 9. 4. The passionate love of God for the evil nation, 9: 10—11: 11. 5. The irrevocable doom, 11: 12—13: 16. 6. Dialogue. The nation's future restoration, 14: 1-9.

QUESTIONS

1. Of which kingdom was Hosea a native? In what contrast does he stand with Amos? In what two periods does his work lie? What was the character of the period following the reign of Jeroboam II.? 2. What tragedy is narrated in the first three chapters? How did this serve to prepare Hosea for his work? What analogy did Hosea's experiences present to those of God? How did the divine message come to complete expression in the life of Hosea? 3. Whom did Hosea blame for the popular irreligion? What was the character of the priests and prophets? How did the princes conduct themselves? What was the character of the government? What was the state of public morals? 4. What are the two contrasting features of Hosea's message? What was his warning to Judah? Did he believe Israel past hope? 5. How do Amos and Hosea reveal the growing power of prophecy? How do they illustrate the advance of prophetic ideals? What is the distinguishing doctrine of Hosea?

CHAPTER VII

ISAIAH: THE PROPHET AS A STATESMAN

1. The religion of Jehovah had always the advantage in the kingdom of Judah after the disruption, for the temple with its imageless worship was in Jerusalem, the capital, and the regular order of services under the Levitical priesthood went on without interruption. At the same time the high places, those ancestral sanctuaries in various parts of the kingdom, retained their popularity and persisted till the time of the great reformation in the reign of Josiah (621 B. C.). But these rural shrines were always in danger of contamination from the proximity of Judah to Israel, where Baal-worship enjoyed royal sanction; and at times this idolatrous cult actually made its way into Jerusalem and was established in the very precincts of the temple. This was true in the reign of Asa (917-876 B. C.), who employed strong measures to remedy it (1 Kings 15:9-14). A similar inroad of heathenism was experienced in the reign of Jehoram (851-843 B. C.), through the influence of his wife Athaliah, a daughter of Ahab and Jezebel; but at her death the city was purified and the temple repaired (2 Kings 11:12). In the reign of Ahaz (735-715 B. C.) other foreign

elements appeared. The horrible rite of human sacrifice, not unknown in earlier periods, and practiced among other nations as a religious custom, was enforced by royal example, and an altar of foreign fashion was introduced into the temple (2 Kings 16:1-4, 10-18). With Hezekiah (715-686 B. C.) a new era of reform was ushered in, suggested and encouraged by the preaching of Isaiah and Micah. After the days of Amos and Hosea the northern kingdom hastened to its fall, and the work of the prophets centered in Judah. In the reformation of Hezekiah the obelisks and images of the heathen worship were overthrown, and the brazen serpent, now become an object of veneration, was destroyed (2 Kings 18:1-5). This king put forth the first effort to destroy the high places, whose evil effects had perhaps already become apparent to the prophets.

2. The work of Isaiah and Micah brought a new influence to bear on the life of Judah. The former seems to have belonged to the higher circles in Jerusalem, and for forty years (737-701 B. C.) was prominent in the political and religious life of the people. He was a man of the city and the court, as his language shows. Micah, on the other hand, was a country man and employs the figures of speech which belong to rural life. With these preachers prophecy reaches its highest level as an effort to save the nation from its sins and their certain consequences. The picture of the times furnished by those

two books is graphic. Foreign relations have brought in manners and customs unsuitable to the people of God. Jerusalem is full of luxury and idols (Isa. 2:5-11). Monopolists, skeptics, perverters of justice and corrupt judges abound (5:12-24). The images, to which Isaiah refers, not so much in wrath as contempt, seem not to have been the representations of other deities, but the means by which the worship of Jehovah was reduced to a mere superstition. The service of the temple was kept up carefully, but it could not be accepted as a substitute for righteousness (Isa. 1:10-17). A striking picture of the situation is presented in chapter 1, which may well be called "The Great Arraignment." Meantime, while Judah was pursuing a career of pride and selfishness, another nation on the eastern horizon was steadily pressing westward, and was destined to play a conspicuous part in the drama of western politics and act as the chastiser of Judah for her forgetfulness of God. That nation was Assyria, some knowledge of whose operations is essential to an understanding of Judah's problems and Isaiah's preaching in this period. In 739 B. C. the Assyrian king Tiglathpileser III. (745-727 B. C.) took the cities of Arpad and Hamath, on the far northeastern frontier, and in 732 B. C. Damascus, the capital of the kingdom of Syria, was captured by him. Ten years later, after a long siege by Shalmaneser IV. (727-722 B. C.), Samaria, the capital of the kingdom of Israel, was conquered by Sargon (722-705 B. C.). A few years later the same king invaded the neighboring district of Philistia (711 B. C.), and in 701 B. C. his successor Sennacherib (705-681 B. C.) was encamped before Jerusalem, demanding its surrender. It was this growing danger from Assyria which formed the background to all Isaiah's preaching. With a vision of the outcome of events which no one about him shared, he preached the necessity of national and individual righteousness, as the only means of escape from the coming disasters. To him the Assyrian was only an instrument in the hand of God (10:5), but unless the nation repented of its sin, the blow must fall.

3. The vision by which Isaiah was called to his prophetic work occurred in 737 B. C., the year of King Uzziah's death (Isa. 6). It gave him the keynote of his message—the holiness of God; and supplied him with a new name for Jehovah—the Holy One of Israel (v. 3), not in the sense of ceremonial separation, but of moral purity and spiritual power (Isa. 1:4; 5:16, 19, 24). The vision of the divine holiness caused him to perceive his own sin (6:5), and the joy of forgiveness issued in an offer of himself for service (vs. 6-8). Thus he was chosen to go and proclaim to Israel the will of God, but was at the same time warned that the result of his preaching would be seemingly only negative and resultless, until the divine chastisements had reduced the nation to a pure remnant (vs. 9-13). Thus began

Isaiah: the Prophet as a Statesman 67

that ministry which continued almost a half-century, and the records of which are contained in the book which bears the prophet's name. It is evident that when the scattered materials recording the life and utterances of Isaiah were collected, either by himself, or some of his intimate friends and disciples (8:16), or perhaps by others living at a later period, they were not arranged in chronological order. Nevertheless, it is quite possible to secure a fairly accurate idea of the course of Isaiah's ministry during the reigns of Jotham, Ahaz and Hezekiah (1:1). He was married, and his wife is once called the "prophetess" (8:3). Two children were born in this family, to both of whom were given symbolical names — Shear Jashub ("the remnant shall return," in allusion to one of the important themes of Isaiah's preaching), and Maher-shalal-hash-baz ("haste booty, speed prey," referring to the Assyrian invasion, upon which the prophet continually insisted). The sermons of the first period, the reign of Jotham (737-735 B. C.), reveal both the corrupt condition of society, enriched during the prosperous times of Uzziah (Azariah), and the prophet's efforts to bring about a better state of society. In the two discourses which belong to this time, the one regarding the exalted mountain (chapters 2-4) and the one on the vineyard (5:1-25; 9:8—10:4; 5:26-30), the true state of affairs is disclosed, and the different abuses which are bringing Judah to ruin are denounced. There is something very modern in this portrayal of evils, for they are the sins of our own day as well as of that—selfishness, intemperance, disbelief, injustice, corruption in official life, and the bad administration of public affairs. Four points appear constantly in Isaiah's preaching—the sin of the nation, the consequent destruction that must come, the escape or survival of the best elements in the state as the seed of the future nation, and the ideal time of peace and righteousness when the darkness is past.

4. The second period of Isaiah's ministry lay in the reign of Ahaz (735-715 B. C.), and witnessed the crisis in the affairs of Judah with reference to Israel and Syria. These two northern kingdoms, witnessing the advance of Assyria toward the west, joined forces for resistance, and endeavored to force Judah to enter the alliance. Isaiah strongly counselled non-interference and quiet as the only safe course. When Ahaz refused to unite with Israel and Syria against Assyria, the two kingdoms entered upon a campaign against Jerusalem (Isa. 7). In this crisis Ahaz was terrified, and instead of heeding Isaiah's advice to remain at rest and keep out of all entanglements, he sent to Assyria and besought its king, Tiglath-pileser, to assist him against his enemies (2 Kings 16:1-9). This plan was effective for the moment, but it involved Judah in relations with the eastern empire which were the cause of numberless disasters in the future. Isaiah foresaw all this, and denounced

Isaiah: the Prophet as a Statesman 69

in unmeasured terms the cowardice and lack of faith displayed by the king, pointing out the fact that within five years his enemies should be destroyed, but that also the wave of Assyrian conquest which he had invited should sweep on into his own land and leave it desolate (7:10-25). These predictions of the fall of Damascus and Samaria were fulfilled to the letter. In the third period of his work, which fell in the reign of Hezekiah (715-686 B. C.), the prophet combated the popular desire for independence. He had held at first to the policy of non-interference and national seclusion; but when the yoke of Assyrian rule was accepted by Ahaz, Isaiah said that any attempt to break away from this obligation would involve Judah in overwhelming difficulties. He, therefore, opposed with all his power that party in the state which advised independence from Assyria and an alliance with Egypt. Hezekiah, though a good king as a ruler, and willing to undertake certain reforms under prophetic guidance, was led at times into foolish conduct involving his kingdom in difficulties. Such acts as the compact with Merodach-baladan of Babylon (chapter 39), and the overtures to Egypt for assistance (chapters 30-32), met the prophet's unmeasured disapproval. His ministry came to its culmination with the great campaign of Sennacherib against Jerusalem. Isaiah had persistently warned the people that God would bring the Assyrians upon them as a punishment for their sins.

To these warnings they were indifferent. But when at last their enemies were actually thundering at the gates of Jerusalem, all eyes turned to the prophet for help. His faith rose serene to meet the emergency. He assured the panic-stricken king and people that God would deliver the city. Nor was he deceived. Some mysterious visitation destroyed a large part of the Assyrian army, and the rest hastily left the country. Thus our last glimpse of the great prophet, reformer, statesman and preacher reveals him as the supreme and commanding spirit in one of the greatest crises of the national life.

5. But it was not with political interests alone that Isaiah concerned himself. He was first and always a preacher of righteousness, interested alike in the religious improvement of the individual and of the state. His supreme purpose was to hasten the arrival of that ideal future to which he confidently looked forward. That time of long prosperity could only come when God had purged away the sin of Jerusalem, by visitations of judgment. Isaiah's great doctrine was that of the "remnant," the righteous stock which would survive the purgation about to come. This idea was as old as the days of Elijah (1 Kings 19:18), but it was developed into an important doctine by Isaiah. Its statement came with his call (6:13); it was given formal embodiment in the name of his elder son (7:3), and was a constituent part of every great utterance

(cf. 4:3; 10:20, etc.). The glorious future which was associated in the prophet's thought with the survival and supremacy of this fittest portion of the nation was the Messianic age, whose blessings were mediated by the Righteous King who should sit on David's throne. This figure of the royal deliverer Isaiah saw with distinctness, though the time and manner of His coming were not so clear. In every dark hour of the national history through the long period of his ministry this was the ever-present vision with which he encouraged the faithful. When Tiglathpileser was ravaging the northern territories, and threatening descent upon the terrified people of Judah, Isaiah spoke confidently of the child-king, the deliverer, whose manifold names of power described his Messianic character (9:1-7). In similar manner he speaks of the divine Branch who is to appear after the land is cleansed (4:2), and of the shoot from the stock of Jesse who was yet to arise with the spirit of wisdom and power, and whose reign should be marked by that era of peace whose fair vision has ever haunted the world since it was uttered by the prophet (11:1-9). This king who was to reign in righteousness (32:1), whose beauty and whose far-stretching land men were to contemplate with wonder, never arose in Judah as an earthly monarch, but these promises were more than fulfilled in the spiritual sovereignty of him whom Pilate called in mockery the king of the Jews, but whose dominion already extends from sea to sea, and from the river to the ends of the earth.*

THE BOOK OF ISAIAH
(The First Part.)

I. The first period (737-732 B. C.); the reign of Jotham.
   1. The call of Isaiah, 6. 2. The exalted mountain, 2-4. The text (2:2-4): idolatry and luxury (vs. 5-11); impending wrath (2:12; 4:1); the glorious future (4:2-6). 3. Sermon of the Vineyard, 5:1-25; 9:8—10:4; 5:26-30 (735-732 B. C.). The parable and its application (5:1-7); monopolists, drunkards, skeptics, perverters, corrupt judges (8-24); judgments already sent; earthquake (25), loss, war, anarchy, defeat (9:8—10:4); the final judgment: Assyria is coming (5:26-30).

II. Second period of Isaiah's ministry (732-711 B. C.); the reign of Ahaz.
   1. Isaiah and Ahaz, 7 (732 B. C.). Message of comfort to the troubled king (7:1-9); the Immanuel sign (10-16); pictures of the coming invasion (17-25). 2. The tablet and the child, 8, 9:1-7 (732 B. C.). The tablet (8:1-4); the river, Assyria (5-8); "God with us" (9-15); a rejected message (16-18); coming gloom (19-22); glorious contrast: the wonderful child (9:1-7). 3. Damascus about to fall, 17:1-11 (732 B. C.). Israel and Judah will also be distressed. 4. Samaria's end at hand, 28 (722

---

* The portion of the book of Isaiah which has been studied in this chapter is the greater part of chapters 1-39, though it has been impossible to consider the national prophecies of Isaiah, chapters 15, 16, 19, 21:1—23:18. Other sections of the book seem to refer to later periods of the history, and will be considered in subsequent chapters, especially chapter 12. Such portions include 13:1—14:23; 34, 35, 40-66 and 24-27.

… B. C.). Drunken leaders of Samaria (1-13); warning to the rulers in Jerusalem (14-29).

III. Third period of Isaiah's ministry (711-701 B. C.); the reign of Hezekiah.
1. The fall of Ashdod predicted, 20 (711 B. C.). The folly of the Egyptian party.
2. Impending fall of Babylon, 21:1-10 (711 B. C.). 3. Illness of Hezekiah, 38 (711 B. C.).
4. Messengers from Babylon, 39 (711 B. C.).
5. The Great Arraignment, 1 (711 B. C.). Wretched condition of Jerusalem (1-9): uselessness of formal worship (10-17); a coming judgment (18-31). 6. The coming siege of Ariel (Jerusalem), 29 (702 B. C.). 7. The folly of reliance on Egypt, 30-32 (702 B. C.). 8. The Assyrian and the future, 10: 5—12: 6 (701 B. C.). Assyria is God's instrument, and will be humbled (10: 5-27); his approach and destruction (28-34); the shoot of Jesse (11: 1-9); the glorious future (11: 10—12: 6). 9. Smitten foes, 14: 24-27; 17: 12-14; 18: 33. 10. The great deliverance, 36, 37 (701 B. C.).

QUESTIONS

1. In which kingdom had the religion of Jehovah the advantage? Why? What was the dangerous element in the popular religion? Who attempted reforms in Judah? 2. What two prophets co-operated during the reign of Hezekiah? How were the two men contrasted? What was the state of affairs in Judah? What was the effect of the temple service upon the religious life of the people? What foreign nation gradually affected the life of Judah? What were the advancing steps of its western conquests? How did these facts enter into the preaching of Isaiah? 3. Describe the vision associated with Isaiah's call. Is the arrangement of the book of Isaiah chronological? What family did Isaiah have? What two discourses are preserved from the reign of Jotham? What sins do they rebuke? 4. What crisis occurred during the reign of Ahaz? What was Isaiah's attitude regarding it? What predictions did he make? How did he change his attitude regarding

an alliance with Assyria? What was the weak element in Hezekiah? What was Isaiah's message at the time of Sennacherib's invasion? 5. What was Isaiah's chief purpose? What was his great doctrine, and what was its meaning? What was his teaching regarding the Messianic king? In whom alone were these promises fulfilled?

CHAPTER VIII

MICAH, THE TRIBUNE OF THE PEOPLE

1. Of the personal life of this contemporary of Isaiah we have almost no information. A single reference to him in Jeremiah's preaching (26:18) shows him to have been a fearless prophet of the days of Hezekiah, and points out the utterance which he most frequently repeated, as a sort of text for his discourses, "Zion shall be plowed as a field, and Jerusalem shall become heaps" (Micah 3:12). The man was not city-born, like Isaiah, but came from Moresheth-Gath, a village in the low country of Judah. Yet his preaching attracted the attention of Hezekiah in the early part of his reign, and was in all probability the foundation of those reforms which he undertook (2 Kings 18:1-8). There is no reason to doubt that the two prophets worked together in the accomplishment of the tasks entrusted to them. This relation is suggested by their common use of the famous passage regarding the mountain of Jehovah's house (Isa. 2:2-4; Mic. 4:1-3), which the younger prophet may have borrowed from his colleague, although it is probable both took it from some otherwise unknown prophecy of an earlier day.

2. Isaiah had spoken of the evils of his time as an interested observer, intent upon pointing out abuses and warning evil-doers,

Micah, however, was a member of the peasant class, and spoke for his fellow countrymen who were suffering under the oppressive social system of the age. This system placed all the power in the hands of a few men, and left to the toilers all the burdens and none of the benefits. It is as a champion of his class as well as a prophet of the Lord that Micah lifts his voice. He was in the truest sense the tribune and defender of the people. The cities, Samaria and Jerusalem, are the centers of this oppressive and unjust arrangement (1:5). The nobility are selfish and overbearing. They plan the seizure of property from the citizens, and carry out their plans, because none are able to oppose them (2:1, 2). Those who have rule actually seem to hate good and love evil. They strip the people of their possessions to such an extent that they seem to flay them alive and eat their flesh (3:1-3). They are building houses in Jerusalem, but they build with blood and iniquity (vs. 9, 10). A poor man can secure no justice in the courts, because the judges take the side of the largest bribes (v. 11). Closely related to such unfaithful and selfish princes and judges were the prophets of the day, the professional religious teachers. Here at last the order had reached the lowest level of subserviency to popular demands for smooth and easy preaching. These men were not likely to arouse the conscience of the nation. Their preaching sounded no note of alarm. Indeed, they were intent solely upon securing their gifts of money, and their indignation was aroused not by the sight of sin, but by the failure of their rewards (3:5, 11). The result is that the people are willing to pay for any kind of preaching which makes no moral demands upon them; they are pleased with lying and licentious teachers rather than with true ones (2:11). Such a condition could not fail to be worse than the total absence of prophecy. Better the old days when the prophets were roving bands of fanatical enthusiasts, with no knowledge but only zeal, than this polished and polite insult to all the nobler ideals of the prophetic work. It was not strange that under such influences the people attempted to silence men like Micah with such words as "Do not prophesy," cease to preach such unwelcome things (2:6). He could only indignantly reply that his words were good to those who walked uprightly (v. 7). The false prophets had no message from God, but he was empowered by the Spirit to speak (3:6-8).

3. There was but one outcome to such conditions—a great national calamity. This was certainly about to overtake Samaria, and could not long be turned aside from Jerusalem (1:6-9; 3:12). But the vision of Micah reaches further apparently than that of Isaiah. The latter expects the time of Messianic blessing in the near future, when the Assyrian has been driven back and Jerusalem delivered. But Micah sees that redemption and peace are to be expected

only after a period of exile in Babylon (4:9, 10). Yet out of this same humiliation is to emerge deliverance, for at the very moment when the nations are triumphing over Zion, a leader of ancient lineage is to arise from Bethlehem Ephrathah and deliver Judah from the Assyrian, who stands for all enemies (4:11; 5:9). Then shall ensue the age of purity, when evils shall be cast out and idolatry at last destroyed (vs. 10-15). Here is seen clearly once more the Messianic hope, and though the vision takes a longer range of time, its issues are the same as in that of Isaiah. The tone of chapters 6, 7, is quite different from the earlier portion of the book, and it has been thought by some that they reflect the dark period of Manasseh, into which Micah may have survived, or are perhaps the work of another and later prophet. They are marked by a far less hopeful feeling, and seem to voice the thought of one who in the midst of gloom could only wait for better days. They contain, however, a passage which is one of the gems of prophecy, worthy to rank with the great utterance of Samuel, "To obey is better than sacrifice" (1 Sam. 15:22), the pregnant word of Hosea which Jesus was accustomed to repeat, "I desire mercy and not sacrifice" (Hos. 6:6; cf. Matt. 9:13; 12:7), the exhortation of Amos, "Let judgment roll down as waters, and righteousness as a mighty stream" (Amos 5:24), or Isaiah's majestic characterization of the qualifications necessary for companionship with God

Micah, the Tribune of the People

(Isa. 33:14-17). It is the prophet's response to the question as to what offerings one must bring to God; shall they be burnt offerings, or calves, thousands of rams, or ten thousands of rivers of oil? Shall it even be a more precious offering, one's first-born child, the fruit of the body for the sin of the soul? To all this the prophetic voice responds in a declaration which in power and beauty approaches the New Testament: "He hath showed thee, O man, what is good; and what doth the Lord require of thee, but to do justly and to love mercy, and to walk humbly with thy God?" (6:8).

THE BOOK OF MICAH

I. The calamity impending over Samaria, in which Jerusalem shall be involved, chap. 1.
  1. The title, 1:1. 2. The Lord is about to visit terrible judgments upon the land, 1:2-4. 3. The cause of this visitation is the sin of Samaria and Jerusalem, 1:5-7. 4. The prophet's distress in view of the coming trouble, 1:8. 5. The fall of Samaria will involve Judah, 1:9. 6. Graphic picture of the fate of towns in the path of the invading Assyrian, 1:10-16.

II. Sins that have brought on this calamity, chaps. 2, 3.
  1. The nobles are greedy and oppressive; they shall be spoiled, 2:1-5. 2. Angry protests against the rebukes of the prophet, 2:6. 3. Reply of Micah that they are responsible, 2:7-10. 4. False prophets the only ones to whom they will listen, 2:11. 5. An abrupt transition; Israel united and victorious under the leadership of God, 2:12, 13. 6. The heartless selfishness of the popular leaders, 3:1-4. 7. In contrast with false prophets, Micah has a divine message, 3:5-8. 8. Crimes of selfish priests and prophets are bringing Jerusalem to ruin, 3:9-12.

III. The promise of restoration and blessing, chaps. 4, 5.
  1. The future exaltation of Mt. Zion, 4: 1-5. 2. In that time God will restore the scattered nation to its home, 4: 6-8. 3. But there will be first a period of distress and exile, 4: 9-10. 4. Then Zion in might will thresh her enemies as sheaves, 4: 11-13. 5. To Israel, insulted by foes, Bethlehem will give the Messianic King, 5: 1-4. 6. Leaders will be found and Assyria shall be punished, 5: 5, 6. 7. The remnant of Jacob, beneficent as dew, strong as a lion, 5: 7-9. 8. The nation transformed; war and idolatry banished, 5: 10-15.
IV. God's controversy with Israel, chaps. 6, 7.
  1. Israel commanded to meet God in judgment; the mountains as witnesses, 6: 1, 2. 2. Jehovah's case stated; His constant care for Israel, 6: 3-5. 3. Israel's awe-stricken question, "What offering will atone?" 6: 6, 7. 4. The answer: "Justice, mercy, humility," 6: 8. 5. Divine denunciation of fraud, oppression, lies, and idolatry, 6: 9-16. 6. Lament of the righteous over the degenerate times, 7: 1-6. 7. In sadness he must wait for better days, 7: 7-10. 8. Prosperity can only come at a distant day, 7: 11-13. 9. The prophet's prayer for the return of the divine presence as in the old time. This alone can bring victory and blessing, 7: 14-20.

QUESTIONS

1. What was the text of Micah's preaching? What was his relation to Isaiah? 2. To what class of society did he belong? How did he represent it? What were his charges against the upper classes? What did he say regarding the prophets of the popular cult? 3. What did he foresee? How does his vision of the future differ from that of Isaiah? Out of what city of Judah was the deliverer to come? In what respect do the closing chapters of the book differ from the earlier ones? What is their most impressive statement? With what other prophetic words may it be compared?

CHAPTER IX

THE PROPHECIES OF NAHUM, ZEPHANIAH, HABAKKUK AND OBADIAH

1. The two kings who followed Hezekiah upon the throne of Judah were Manasseh (686-641 B. C.), and Amon (641-639 B. C.), and during their reigns the true religion suffered an almost total eclipse. The narrative of this period is contained in 2 Kings 21, and shows that the influences which surrounded Manasseh in his youth must have inclined him strongly toward heathenism. All the abominations which his father had banished from Judah were restored; the high places were established, the worship of Baal and Astarte, the cruel and licentious cult of Phœnicia, was introduced once more, various forms of magic and divination were employed by the king, new types of idolatry from the east were brought in, and even human sacrifice was sanctioned by the royal example. But Manasseh was not satisfied to become an apostate himself; he sought to compel all his people to forsake the religion of Isaiah and Micah. A great persecution was waged against the faithful, so that the martyrs to the cause of righteousness were a great host. Tradition has asserted that Isaiah was sawn asunder among these victims of Manasseh's fury (cf. Heb. 11:37). The writer of Chronicles asserts that for

these sins the heathenizing king was punished by an invasion of the Assyrian army, and imprisonment in Babylon, which led to his repentance and restoration (2 Chr. 33:11-20). But his change of conduct came too late in his reign to seriously modify the effects of his conduct, and his son Amon followed his evil example. Thus for a full half-century the worship of Jehovah was placed under ban and the voice of prophecy was almost hushed. But with the accession of Josiah (639-609 B. C.) there came a change. He had been educated under the influence of the God-fearing party at the court, and was open to the leadership of the priests and prophets who speedily asserted their power. By his direction the temple was cleansed and repaired, and in the process a book of law was found, which is usually supposed to have been the book of Deuteronomy (2 Kings 22:3-10). Surprised and alarmed by the regulations laid down in this book, Josiah instantly began a general reformation in accordance with the newly discovered law (2 Kings 22:11—23:25). His untimely death soon after caused a reaction and left the reforming party without a leader; and from that time to the close of Judah's history as a kingdom the descent was rapid (2 Kings 23:29, 30).

2. Nahum was the first prophet to break the long silence. Somewhere in the earlier portion of the reign of Josiah his book seems to belong, and may be dated perhaps 625 B. C. Its theme is the approaching fall of

Nineveh, the capital of Assyria. This was the nation that had held the mastery of the world for centuries, crushing the nations with remorseless barbarity under its feet. Time after time its armies had swept westward across the Euphrates and devastated the coast lands. Tiglathpileser had conquered Damascus in 732 B. C.; Shalmaneser had besieged Samaria, and Sargon had at last destroyed it in 722 B. C.; Sennacherib had plundered Judah and only been prevented from taking Jerusalem by a providential interference in 701 B. C., and what these western nations had suffered at the hands of this proud and cruel people was but an example of the devastation which followed their forces on every side. But the day of retribution was at hand. The race whose career had been one long drama of bloodshed and oppression, and whose repentance (Jonah 3:4-10), if actual, was but brief, was at last to suffer at the hands of Nabopolassar, who, with the combined troops of the Medes and Babylonians, took Nineveh in 607 B. C., and established the empire of Babylonia on the ruins of Assyria. Thus nearly a score of years before the event, the inspired prophet predicted the downfall of the oppressive city. The book opens with a majestic reference to the power of Jehovah, who rules among the nations according to His will. Then the prophet plunges into his theme, the impotence of those who afflict the chosen nation to stand before the divine wrath (1:7-11). Then in graphic terms the coming siege of Nineveh is described; the preparations for battle (2:3-5); the strengthening of the walls (3:14); then the catastrophe by which the rising of the Tigris is said to have aided the attacking force (2:6); the contrast of the past power of the city whose emblem was a lion with the ruined condition after the siege (2:11), when the triumphant chariots of the conquerors drive remorselessly over the heaps of slain (3:1-3). Assyria was growing weak, her princes were not watchful (3:18), therefore she should fall. She boasted of her strength, but so had No-Amon (Thebes) in Egypt, which Ashurbanipel took in 662 B. C. (3:8-11). But the prophet's purpose is not merely that of prediction for its own sake. His message is one of comfort to his people, so long harassed by Assyria. This foe shall afflict them no more (1:12, 13). Thus the message of this otherwise unknown man of God from the little town of Elkosh in southern Judah finds an important place among the utterances of the Old Testament.

3. Zephaniah has taken pains to trace his genealogy back to Hezekiah, who may be no other than the king of that name (Zeph. 1:1). The prophecy was probably uttered about 625 B. C. The leading event of this portion of the reign of Josiah was the invasion of the western lands by a vast host of Scythians, wild horsemen, who, like the Huns of later days, spread terror before them and left ruin behind. It is not probable that Judah was actually overrun by these bar-

Four of the Minor Prophets

barians, but the universal alarm caused by their presence in Syria and their raids along the Mediterranean coast gave the prophet his theme—the coming day of destruction for Judah, still under the influence of the long idolatry of Manasseh's reign. "The great day of the Lord" (1:14) formed the subject of the prophet's thought, and passed over into mediæval poetry in the great hymn, "Dies iræ, dies illa." Sweeping destruction is about to fall, in which men and animals shall perish. Judah and Jerusalem are to suffer, and false worshipers, waverers, apostates and the indifferent shall be destroyed (1:2-6). The sins of the time are rapacity and dishonesty. Jerusalem is to be searched and the arrogant rich despoiled (1:9-13). Because of such sins the day of the Lord is near. This expression passed easily into later prophecy, and came to stand for any divine visitation. Sin must be purged away by chastisement. The time of chastisement, whenever it might come, was the day of the Lord. It was a day of judgment, and though often repeated, it was always a symbol of the great day of judgment at the end of all. The call to escape is followed by a list of the nations that shall suffer for their sins, among which Assyria appears (2:4-15). Here, as in Amos, the catalogue of nations who shall suffer is but the prelude to the announcement of Jerusalem's punishment, because she is proud, oppressive and disobedient; her rulers are avaricious and rapacious, and her religious leaders pervert their office. Jehovah has given ample instruction, yet no attention is paid to it, and examples of national disaster have been furnished without result (3:1-7). The closing part of the book is more hopeful. There are some righteous remaining among the people. To these the prophet speaks encouragingly, bidding them wait till the purification is accomplished, after which the nations shall speak a pure speech, offerings shall be brought from afar to Jehovah, the proud shall be removed, the humble alone remaining, and the purified Israel shall be righteous and secure (3:9-13). The message closes with the rejoicing of the true Israel. The emphasis of Zephaniah is upon the certainty of divine wrath against sin, but also the redemptive character of its penalties, with the further thought that redemption includes not only Israel, but all nations.

4. Habakkuk is another of the prophets regarding whom we have absolutely no knowledge beyond the title of the book. One could wish to know more of these men who have left only the briefest utterances from what may have been lives full of prophetic activity. We can only be grateful that in the providence of God something, and we may trust the best, of their messages has survived. The situation revealed in the book of Habakkuk is fairly clear. It was probably the change which came over the politics of the world by the fall of Nineveh and the rise of Babylon in

Four of the Minor Prophets

607 B. C. which supplied the motive for this prophetic word. Nineveh, the oppressor, had fallen, as both Nahum and Zephaniah foresaw. But had anything been gained by the transfer of power from one nation to another equally unscrupulous? Was it not as hard a fate to be under the dominion of the Chaldeans (Babylonians) as of the Assyrians? These were the new foes whose power was threatening Judah in the closing years of Josiah, and after his death. How could the divine purpose be justified in the presence of such events? This is the problem which finds expression in the book. It was probably written shortly before the battle of Carchemish in 604 B. C., in which the supremacy of Babylonia over Egypt and all the western lands was decided. The prophecy is in the form of a dialogue between the prophet and God. The former complains that his people are in distress because of the violence and injustice which they suffer (1:2-4). The divine voice replies that a strange thing is about to happen. God is soon to raise up the proud and conquering Chaldeans as his instruments of vengeance (1:5-11). The prophet anxiously inquires how God can use such a ruthless instrument. Can He permit such a barbarous people to execute His will (vs. 12-17)? The prophet pauses for the divine answer, which comes at last in the form of an oracle: "The Chaldean is indeed puffed up with pride; but the just shall be preserved by his faithfulness" (2:4). In this word is found

the secret of comfort. God's purposes may be mysterious, but His people must wait in confidence. The righteous man saves himself by trusting Jehovah. The prophet then comments on the oracle which has come to him, and on the character of the Chaldeans, but feels assured at last that God rules, and the earth must keep silence before him (2:20). The closing section (chapter 3) is an ode whose theme is confidence in God and in His power and willingness to aid His people. Thus the problem of doubt, which baffled and perplexed so many godly souls amid the distresses of these and later unhappy years, was answered by the call to lean upon God, and trust Him to the end.

5. Obadiah, whose book would naturally fall to be considered somewhat later, but is inserted here for convenience of grouping, has left a single short yet most expressive utterance dealing with a theme never forgotten in the dark days which followed the fall of Jerusalem and the beginning of the Exile. The relations between Israel and the Edomites were never friendly. These descendants of Esau dwelt in the rocky country, south and east of the Dead Sea, and at various times there had been war between them and Israel (2 Sam. 8:14; 2 Kings 8:20-22; 14:7; 2 Chr. 25:11, 12). The ill feeling between the two nations, and especially the vindictive hatred and cruelty of Edom, are abundantly witnessed in the Old Testament, calling from the prophets denunciations upon these rock dwellers for

their fierce deeds of blood (Amos 1:11, 12; Jer. 49:7-22; Ezek. 25:12-14; 35). That which constituted the chief offense of the Edomites in the eyes of the people of Judah, and to which several of these prophecies distinctly refer, was the savage joy with which they hailed the destruction of Jerusalem and added their taunts to the sorrows of the unhappy Jews. The exiles in Babylon could not forget this inhuman conduct (Ps. 137:7), and among the hopes cherished by even the most pious of Israel was the expectation that the future Deliverer of the nation would come to His kingdom with garments dyed red with the blood of Edom (Isa. 63:1-6). This coming vengeance upon the hated race is the theme of Obadiah. Whether the fragment was written shortly after the downfall of Jerusalem in 586 B. C. or in some later period of the history it is perhaps impossible to determine, but it recalls vividly the conduct of these foes of Judah in that awful time of her distress, when they watched exultantly the progress of her humiliation and were as one of her enemies (v. 11), or cut off the stragglers and those who attempted to escape (v. 14). For all this, says the prophet, the "day of the Lord" is sure to dawn for Edom, and though the rock fastnesses in which they hide be strong and apparently inaccessible, they shall be brought down and their treasures carried away (vs. 3, 4, 6, 8, 15). If the tone of Obadiah and other prophecies of vengeance upon the enemies of Israel seem to us harsh and vindictive, we must bear in mind the age in which they were uttered; the large element of race prejudice and hatred which characterized Israel as well as the other nations, from which even the prophets were not free; the identification of these heathen nations in the minds of the prophets with the wicked and idolatrous forms of life which the chosen people must be taught to hate and avoid; and, further, the fact that our ability to discern the imperfect and unspiritual character of such utterances is the result of our education in the school of the Master, in comparison with whom even the greatest of the prophets were but partial and imperfect interpreters of truth.

THE BOOK OF NAHUM

I. The divine avenger, chap. 1.
   1. The title, 1:1.   2. The power of God to chastise His enemies, 1:2-10.   3. A word of comfort to Judah in view of the approaching fall of Assyria, 1:11-13.   4. The threat of vengeance upon Nineveh, 1:14.   5. Encouragement to Judah, 1:15.
II. The fall of Nineveh, chap. 2.
   1. Nineveh warned that her enemies are approaching and that Judah is to be vindicated, 2:1, 2.   2. Preparations for the siege 2:3-5.   3. The overthrow of the city, 2:6, 7.   4. Flight of her defenders, 2:8.   5. The spoiling of the city, 2:9-13.
III. The sins for which punishment must come, chap. 3.
   1. Destruction coming because of cruelty, falsehood, lust and superstition, 3:1-4.   2. The divine anger, 3:5, 6.   3. Her fall will astonish all, 3:7.   4. Thebes was powerful, yet she fell, 3:8-10.   5. So shall Nineveh fall, 3:11, 12.

6. Prepare for the siege, 3: 13-15. 7. Though rich and powerful, Assyria cannot survive, 3: 16-19.

THE BOOK OF ZEPHANIAH

I. The coming day of wrath, chap. 1.
   1. Title, 1: 1. 2. Destruction about to fall, especially on Jerusalem, 1: 2-6. 3. Jehovah's banquet of vengeance, 1: 7, 8. 4. The doom of dishonest dealers, 1: 9-13. 5. The great day of the Lord, 1: 14-18.
II. Judgments on evil nations and cities, 2: 1—3: 7.
   1. Escape while there is time, 2: 1-3. 2. Philistia, Moab, Ammon, and even distant nations like Ethiopia and Assyria, shall suffer, 2: 4-15. 3. Jerusalem does not profit by these warnings to others, 3: 1-7.
III. The promise of future blessing, 3: 8-20.
   1. Consolation found in waiting, 3: 8. 2. The era of good to come, 3: 9-13. 3. The rejoicing of true Israel, 3: 14-17. 4. Restoration, vindication, glorification, 3: 18-20.

THE BOOK OF HABAKKUK

I. The dialogue between the prophet and God, chaps. 1, 2.
   1. Title, 1: 1. 2. The prophet's cry of despair, 1: 2-4. 3. The divine response; judgment is near, 1: 5-11. 4. The prophet's anxious question: "Will God use the Chaldeans?" 1: 12-17. 5. A pause; the prophet waits the divine response, 2: 1. 6. It comes in the oracle, 2: 2-4. 7. The prophet's comment on the oracle, 2: 5-20.
II. An Ode: "Confidence in God."
   1. Title, 3: 1. 2. Disquieted by the oracle, he asks mercy for Judah, 3: 2. 3. A vision: God's majestic manifestation, and an explanation of the divine purpose, the destruction of the foes of His people, 3: 3-15. 4. In the midst of perplexity the prophet must wait, trusting in God, 3: 16-19.

THE BOOK OF OBADIAH

1. Edom, though proud, shall fall, 1-4. 2. She shall be utterly stripped and forsaken of her allies, 5-7. 3. Her celebrated wisdom shall not save her, 8, 9. 4. Acts of cruelty to Judah for which she is to be punished, 10-16. 5. Judah shall return to her land and chastise Edom, 17-21.

QUESTIONS

1. What was the state of affairs during the reigns of Manasseh and Amon? What was the condition of the prophets and the pious generally during this time? What effect did the repentance of Manasseh have? With whose accession to the throne was there a change? What book was discovered in the temple? What was the character of the reform undertaken? 2. What is the theme of Nahum's prophecy? What was the cause of Assyria's coming destruction? How was this prophecy fulfilled? What was Nahum's purpose in writing? 3. What historical event supplied the motive of Zephaniah's book? What is its theme? For what sins was Jerusalem rebuked? What hopeful features are added in the closing part? 4. What were the events which gave rise to the words of Habakkuk? What was the problem which confronted the prophet? What was the oracle by which he was comforted? 5. In what later time does the prophecy of Obadiah lie? Against what nation does he speak? What were their offenses? How may such utterances be justified?

CHAPTER X

JEREMIAH, THE MARTYR PROPHET

1. There is no career which is more intimately interwoven with the history of Judah in the closing period of the monarchy than that of Jeremiah. If Hosea may be called the prophet of the last days of the kingdom of Israel, certainly Jeremiah is worthy the title of prophet of the decline and fall of Judah. His ministry extended over half a century (1:2, 3), from the middle of Josiah's reign until after the fall of Jerusalem (627-577 B. C.). He was of priestly family, and his home was at Anathoth, a town in the territory of Benjamin (1:1). He was yet but a young man when called to the prophetic office (1:6), and was never married (16:1), but devoted himself continuously to his difficult task, living probably for the most of the time at Jerusalem. When he began his preaching, in the thirteenth year of Josiah, it was in obedience to the divine call which appointed him to act as God's messenger, not alone to Judah, but the nations, "to pluck up and to destroy and to overthrow; to build and to plant," indicating that before there could be true prosperity there must be the judgment upon sin. These were the days in which the irreligious and demoralizing tendencies of the reigns of Manasseh and Amon were still dominant, and the lot

of the prophet of Jehovah was not enviable. His sermons of this period (chapters 1-6) arraign the nation for having exchanged its God for creatures that are no gods, and for listening to prophets who preach the heathen cult (2:8-11; 5:30, 31). The people have not profited by the fearful example of Israel's overthrow because of sin, but seem anxious to outdo the northern kingdom in idolatry (3:6f.), and their gods are as numerous as their cities (2:28). Only destruction could be the result of such disregard of God's will, and the prophet, who loved Jerusalem as his own soul, was distressed at what he foresaw but could not prevent (4:19-22). He could only stand and call the nation back to the old paths which the earlier prophets had pointed out as the true ways of prosperity (6:16).

2. In the year 621 B. C., the eighteenth year of Josiah's reign, a law-book was found in the temple during the progress of repairs ordered by the king. The discovery led to a general attempt at reformation on the part of the king and his priestly and prophetic advisers, among whom Jeremiah seems to have had a place. The words of "this covenant" (2 Kings 23:2, 4) were read before a great assembly of the people, and there was apparently an effort to teach the newly discovered institutes throughout the cities of Judah, an effort in which Jeremiah joined (11:1-3, 6). This period in which the earnest young king was endeavoring to purify his land of idolatry and organize the

worship in conformity with the Deuteronomic law must have been the happiest time in Jeremiah's life. Nevertheless, the task was not easy, and the tide of idolatry which had been growing for half a century could not be checked at once. Jeremiah found the people far from responsive to his preaching, in spite of his royal friend (11:9, 10), and against the prophet himself a murderous plot was set on foot by the men of Anathoth, his own town (11:19-23). But these troubles were inconsiderable as compared with those which the death of Josiah brought upon the reforming party. The king, relying over-confidently upon the divine protection, thrust himself into a quarrel that was not his own by trying to stop the king of Egypt on his way north to contend with the king of Assyria at the Euphrates. He lost his life in a battle or parley (2 Kings 23:29-31), and this fact not only deprived the reformers of their leader and protector, but seemed to set the seal of divine disapproval upon their labors. A relapse into heathenism and immorality rapidly followed. The people of Jerusalem put Jehoahaz, a son of Josiah, upon the throne; but after only three months the king of Egypt, now the master of Judah, removed him in chains to Egypt, and set his brother Eliakim on the throne, changing his name to Jehoiakim. This was the beginning of the lifelong martyrdom of Jeremiah. It was his unhappy fortune to be set to proclaim that Judah's day of salvation was passed, and that nothing remained for her but captivity (chapters 7-10). He realized the burden of his mission sorely (9:1, 2). He saved himself with difficulty from another plot against his life (chapter 26). He felt the tragedy of the removal of Jehoahaz to die in Egypt; and bade the people cease weeping for the dead (Josiah), but to mourn for him who was carried away to return no more (22:10-12).

3. Jeremiah stood practically alone as God's representative in a time of almost total apostasy. He was surrounded by plenty of prophets, but they were the smooth, easy-going, popular, professional preachers whose words awakened no conscience, and who assured the people that the nation was safe in the protecting care of God. This was a true message in Isaiah's day, but that time was long since past, and Jerusalem was destined for captivity. Thus Jeremiah was doomed to preach an unwelcome message, while the false prophets persuaded the people that he was unpatriotic, uninspired and pessimistic (14: 13, 14). This made his task almost too difficult to endure. His cries of anguish are pathetic at times (15:20, 15-18; 20:14-18). At other times, however, when his enemies set in motion devices against him, he broke out into a storm of fury, and poured forth maledictions upon them (18:18-23). Even his patient nature turned at last against such slander and opposition. Once he said he would utterly cease to speak in the name of God;

but the divine word was a fire within his bones, and he could not restrain it (20:7-9). His relations with Jehoiakim the king (609-597 B. C.) were not friendly, and he rarely endangered his life by visiting the court. But in the fifth year of this reign he sent his faithful servant Baruch to read from a roll containing the substance of the prophet's preaching concerning the sins of Judah and neighboring nations; this reading, which took place at the temple on the occasion of a public fast, attracted the attention of the nobles, who invited Baruch to come to the palace and read it to them, which he did. The words of the scroll which the prophet had dictated filled them with such alarm that they resolved to call the attention of the king to the matter. But he, on hearing a part of the messages read, seized the roll, cut it into shreds and threw it into the flames, in spite of the protests of some of his officers. But the attempt of the king to arrest Jeremiah and Baruch was foiled (chapter 36), and another roll which was prepared added a prophetic denunciation of Jehoiakim himself (36:27-32). His reign was followed by that of his son Jehoiachin (Jeconiah or Coniah), who, Jeremiah declared, should be cast out childless and despised (22:24-30). These words were fulfilled only too soon. Nebuchadrezzar, king of Babylon, who by the defeat of the king of Egypt at Carchemish in 604 B. C., predicted in graphic words by Jeremiah (46:2-12), became lord of all the western lands, had found both Jehoiakim and his son inclined to disloyalty (2 Kings 24:1), and resolved to teach Jerusalem a lesson, which he did by removing the king and royal family, together with many of the leading citizens, artisans and soldiers, to the number of ten thousand, to Babylon, leaving the king's uncle, Mattaniah, whose name he changed to Zedekiah, as king (2 Kings 24:8-17). The words of the prophet were speedily being fulfilled.

4. Such was the blindness of the people, however, that they persuaded themselves, in accordance with the words of the false prophets, that the worst was over and that since the city had not been destroyed and the temple was still standing, the captivity of those who had been carried away would soon come to an end, and they would be restored. Against this opinion Jeremiah set himself to preach insistently (chapter 28). He declared that their troubles were but begun, that the temple should fall and its vessels be taken to Babylon. This he did in the interest of peace, and to keep his people from the folly of revolt (27:12-22). He even wrote to those who had been taken to the east, counselling them to be quiet in their new homes, to rear families, acquire possessions and seek the peace of the land, for it would be seventy years before the exile should end (chapter 29). Zedekiah, the last king of Judah, was much more friendly to Jeremiah than Jehoiakim had been, regarding him with mingled reverence and fear. But he was restrained from any open display

of consideration by the hostility of the court
to the prophet. When the king sent to inquire as to the future fate of Judah, Jeremiah
frankly assured him that there was no hope
of independence. Rebellion would bring
disaster. Jerusalem would fall into the
hands of the king of Babylon, and court and
people be carried away. He counselled,
therefore, a peaceful submission, and advised
against any attempt at revolt. But the
folly of the court led the king to disregard
the counsel of the prophet and rebel, trusting
in the support of Egypt. This conduct
brought the forces of Nebuchadrezzar
against the city, and Jeremiah warned the
king that defense was useless (chapter
21). However, an earnest effort was
made to save the kingdom from overthrow;
the defenses of the city were strengthened,
and, as an act likely to secure the favor of
God, all the slaves were set free. There
was indeed a momentary gleam of hope, for
the Egyptians actually made an effort to aid
their allies; and hearing of the approach of
the Pharaoh with his army, the Babylonian
king abandoned the siege. But there was
an instant relapse into the old practices as
soon as the danger seemed averted. The
slaves were once more reduced to their old
position, and affairs went on as before.
Jeremiah denounced this act of perfidy and
injustice, and assured the king that the
respite was but for a moment; the king of
Egypt would return to his own country, and
the Babylonians would renew the siege

(34:8-22; 37:1-10). During this interval Jeremiah attempted to pay a visit to his home at Anathoth, but his departure was mistaken for desertion to the Babylonians, and he was scourged and put into prison (37:11-15). Here the king consulted him in secret, only to be once more assured of the certain destruction of Jerusalem; at the same time the prophet was removed to a more endurable place of confinement (vs. 16-21). But the courtiers could not forgive what they regarded as his unpatriotic conduct, and his life was saved only by the assistance of a servant (chapter 38). He still maintained his attitude of unwavering confidence both in the certainty that Jerusalem should fall, and that later on it should be restored, to which faith he gave expression by the purchase of a plot of land at Anathoth, when the terror of coming destruction was making all property in Judah worthless (chapter 32).

5. To this unhappy period belong some of the most precious of Jeremiah's utterances. When he could no longer preach publicly, he wrote (30:1, 2). He speaks sadly of the distress which disobedience has brought upon Judah, of the hopelessness of any other remedy than exile, and of the heart-breaking bitterness of this experience, in which Rachel, the ancestress of the people and the representative of the motherhood of Judah, weeps for her departing children, and refuses to be comforted (31:15f.). Yet this is but one side of the shield. The exile is not an

end, but only a means of purification. The nation shall return and be re-established; houses shall be built and vineyards planted; a new and spiritual covenant shall be made with the people; the promises made to the fathers shall be fulfilled, and the righteous king of David's line shall reign over a restored and happy people (32:36-44; 33). Out of this dark moment of the nation's life, when hope seemed past, the Messianic promise is uttered with serene confidence in its realization. The final tragedy of the kingdom hastened to its accomplishment. Nebuchadrezzar returned shortly, took Jerusalem, put many of its people to the sword, destroyed it and the temple with fire, and after subjecting Zedekiah to the usual cruelties, he transported him with his court and great numbers of the better class of citizens to Babylon, leaving only a broken and impoverished remnant to mourn over the fallen fortunes of the fair city (chapters 39, 52). The prophet, whose opposition to the foolish policy of revolt had come to the ears of the officers of Nebuchadrezzar, was given the privilege of going with the exiles or remaining with the remnant in Jerusalem. Though there seemed little choice, he preferred to remain (40:1f.). A governor, Gedaliah, was left in charge of the survivors in Judah, and presently a semblance of order began to appear, only to be dissipated by the cruel murder of the deputy by an adventurer named Ishmael (chapters 40, 41). In this emergency, fearing the further wrath of the king of Babylon, a company of the people resolved to make their escape into Egypt as offering some promise of protection. The prophet vainly sought to dissuade them, and was at last compelled to accompany the refugees to their asylum in the south (chapters 42, 43). Here he continued his efforts to keep the people from that idolatry which had been the cause of Judah's downfall; but his words were unheeded, and in our last view of him he is seen warning his obstinate countrymen that the hand of Babylonian chastisement shall reach them even in Egypt (chapter 44). There, amid the mournful surroundings of persistent idolatry and cold indifference to the divine message, with the memory of a lifelong martyrdom, and the vision of a ruined and desolate fatherland ever in his mind, the sad yet majestic man of God waited the last act of the tragedy, the death by stoning at the hands of his own ungrateful people, as Jewish tradition asserts. Few prophets, perhaps none, have ever performed so difficult a task as his. With a sensitive nature that shrunk from misunderstanding and calumny, he was evermore the bearer of unhappy and reproving messages. Yet with fidelity and rare heroism he responded to the voice of God, and has passed into history as one of the choicest spirits of Israel's life, a not unworthy type of the world's redeemer, the suffering Servant of God.

Jeremiah, the Martyr Prophet

THE BOOK OF JEREMIAH

I. First period, in the reign of Josiah (628-609 B. C.).
   1. The call and preaching of Jeremiah before the finding of the law in 621 B. C., chaps. 1-6. 2. Preaching the new law, 11:1-8. 3. The difficulties of the task, 11:9-23; 12: 1-6.

II. Second period, the reign of Jehoiakim (609-597 B. C.).
   1. The relapse into idolatry after the death of Josiah, chaps. 7-10. 2. The plot against Jeremiah, chap. 26. 3. Denunciation of Jehoiakim, 22: 1-19. 4. A drought, the sign of divine displeasure, chaps. 14, 15. 5. The potter's wheel and the prophet's danger, chap. 18. 6. The bottle and the message, 19: 1—20: 18. 7. Coming disasters, chap. 25. 8. The lesson of the Rechabites, chap. 35. 9. Jeremiah's words to Baruch, chap. 45. 10. Prophecies against Egypt, Philistia, Moab, Ammon, Edom, Damascus, and Kedar, 46: 1—49: 33. 11. Jeremiah's roll, chap. 36.

III. The brief reign of Jehoiachin (597 B. C.).
   1. The girdle and its meaning, chap. 13. 2. The rejection of Jehoiachin (Coniah), 22: 20-30.

IV. The reign of Zedekiah (597-586 B. C.).
   1. The future fall of Babylon, chaps. 50, 51. 2. Prophecy against Edom, 49: 34-39. 3. False prophets and worthless people, chaps. 23, 24. 4. Jeremiah's advice to Zedekiah, and to the exiles, chaps. 27-29. 5. Other messages to the king, chap. 21; 34: 1-7. 6. The slaves released and reclaimed, 34: 8-22. 7. Jeremiah's arrest and imprisonment, chaps. 37, 38. 8. The prophet's book, the new covenant, chaps. 30, 31. 9. Jeremiah's purchase of land, chap. 32. 10. The new nation and the Messianic hope, chap. 33. 11. The fall of Jerusalem, chaps. 39, 52.

V. Closing days.
   1. The appointment of Gedaliah as governor, and his murder, chaps. 40, 41. 2. Journey of

many of the Jews into Egypt, with Jeremiah, chaps. 42, 43. 3. The prophet's last message, a protest against the idolatry of the Jews in Egypt, chap. 44.

QUESTIONS

1. Over what periods did the ministry of Jeremiah extend? What is known of his family and home? When did his work begin? 2. What bearing did the discovery of the law book have upon the program of the reformers? What did Jeremiah do during this period? What tragedy deprived him of royal protection? 3. What was Jeremiah's complaint regarding the prophets of the period? What was his message concerning Jerusalem? How was he regarded? How did the king treat his writings? What was the fate of Jehoiachin? 4. What was the false confidence of the people? What did Jeremiah teach regarding Jerusalem? What did he counsel? What befell the city? 5. How was Jeremiah treated? What teachings came from the period of Jeremiah's imprisonment? Who was left as governor after the fall of Jerusalem? What became of Jeremiah after the fall of Gedaliah?

CHAPTER XI

EZEKIEL, THE SHEPHERD OF THE EXILES

1. The period of the exile extended from 586 B. C., the year in which Jerusalem was destroyed by Nebuchadrezzar, to 538 B. C., when Cyrus conquered Babylon and issued the edict permitting the Jews to return to their country. Thus its precise limits scarcely exceeded half a century. But the first deportation took place several years before the city fell, and the return from captivity was slow and partial, continuing for many years after permission was granted; so that Jeremiah's prediction of the period of sojourn in Babylon as seventy years (Jer. 25:11; 29:10), though it was a common Jewish measure of any considerable length of time, was approximately correct. During this time the center of thought was removed from Judah to Babylonia. The temple was demolished and the forms of worship discontinued. The exiles were settled in groups in various parts of the empire, and were permitted to preserve a semblance of their old type of government under elders, the leaders of local communities. Here such religious services as could be carried on apart from any temple or altar worship were preserved, especially by those who retained their interest in the religion of their fathers. Priests and prophets there

were in considerable numbers; but the one man who did most to keep alive the interest of his people in Jehovah was Ezekiel. In a time of false hope in an early return to Jerusalem, of failure to comprehend the greatness and power of God, of danger lest the people should lapse into the heathenism by which they were surrounded, and of growing indifference to the national mission as a prophetic race, he stood almost a solitary figure, speaking in behalf of the true God, and proclaiming both the need of national discipline and the certainty of national restoration.

2. In the first deportation, which took place some eleven years before the city finally fell and in which Jehoiachin was carried away, there came to Babylon this young man of priestly family, and perhaps also of some priestly experience at the temple. The company of which Daniel and his three friends were members seems to have been brought to Babylon at a still earlier period. That Ezekiel had to some extent come under the influence of Jeremiah seems probable. He was taken with a company of the exiles to Tel-Abib, a place on the Chebar, probably one of the canals of southern Babylonia (3:15). He was married, and possessed a house here (24:18; 3:24; 12:7), but beyond this nothing is known of his circumstances. Five years later he was called to the prophetic work by a vision of the glory of God, whose meaning was the omnipresence of the divine power as an

answer to the too prevalent idea that Jehovah was localized in Judah, and unable to assist His people in Babylon. Ezekiel was commissioned to be a watchman to the house of Israel, to speak to the people in behalf of God. They were possessed of the confident expectation that the period of their stay in Babylon was short. The prophets in their midst insisted that they should soon go back. Jerusalem was still standing, and Jeremiah was at that very moment endeavoring to persuade both his fellow citizens in Judah, and the exiles by letter, that the city must fall. This, then, became the task of Ezekiel at Tel-Abib. In this attempt to disillusion his fellow exiles, Ezekiel was instructed to use various symbolic forms of teaching. He depicted a siege on a tile to impress the coming fate of Jerusalem (4:1-3); he ate coarse food and drank water measured out with care, referring to the scantiness of supplies in the coming distress of the distant city (4:9-11); he shaved off his hair and beard, and divided the hair into three parts to denote the various experiences of those in the siege (5:1-4); he gave expression to grief (6:11-21); he moved his household goods (12:1-11); and by a variety of other symbols he set forth the fate of Jerusalem, whose certain destruction he wished to impress upon his incredulous people. He also employed parables to set before them the historical reasons which made necessary the exile, and which now required its more complete manifestation in the total overthrow of

Jerusalem, no longer to be averted. Such parables were those of the vine, the eagle and the cedar, the lioness, and the two sisters (chapters 15, 17, 19, 23).

3. Fortunately, the writings of Ezekiel are not only dated according to the year of his captivity, but they are arranged in chronological order, so that it is possible to observe the progress of events without rearrangement. In this they differ from the writings of Isaiah and Jeremiah. The book of Ezekiel falls into three divisions. The first (chapters 1-24) is occupied with his messages to the Jews in Babylon prior to the fall of Jerusalem, of whose certainty he vainly sought to convince them. In this portion of his ministry he seems to have been regarded with little confidence or favor. He was occasionally consulted, at his home by the elders of the community (14:1f.; 20:1f.), but although they regarded him as a prophet, they preferred to follow the leadership of those teachers who spoke a more pleasing message, and whom Ezekiel denounced as false prophets (chapter 13); while the people at large regarded him as a mere speaker of parables (20:49). But the prophet knew whereof he spoke. He was made aware of the real conditions prevailing at Jerusalem. In visions granted alone to a true prophet he saw the image of the obscene goddess Astarte set up and worshiped in the very precincts of the temple, while other forms of idolatry, such as the worship of beasts, the mourning for Tammuz and sun-worship,

together with various sorts of divination, showed the utterly corrupt character of a majority of the people (chapter 8). Nothing but destruction remained for such a worthless nation (chapter 9), and it was not strange that the vision was completed by the departure of the divine glory from the doomed sanctuary (11:23). Ezekiel showed his countrymen that the occasion of the exile was not alone the sin of past generations, but of the present. Every man was responsible for himself and his own conduct, not for the deeds of his ancestors (chapter 18). Thus, the doctrine of individual responsibility reached its full statement through these great prophets of the decline and fall of Judah, Jeremiah and Ezekiel. Though the latter never strikes the deep notes of tenderness sounded by Hosea and Jeremiah, he asserts repeatedly the fact that God has no pleasure in the death of him that dieth; His will is that the sinner shall turn to Him and live. The way of obedience is clearly pointed out, whereby one may find God and salvation (18:5-9); nor is this path one of mere ceremonial righteousness, but rather of moral likeness to God. In such words Isaiah seems to speak afresh.

4. In the second section of the book (chapters 25-32) the prophet describes the woes that shall fall upon the nations which have oppressed Israel or are now glorying in her downfall. Although she is suffering, it is not theirs to rejoice in her calamity. These oracles were apparently written dur-

ing two years of comparative silence, after Ezekiel received intimation that the final siege of Jerusalem had actually begun (24:1, 2). He was told at the same time that he would receive word of the fall of the city from a refugee, and meantime he should remain quiet (vs. 25-27). He, therefore, took up the story of the nations which had contributed to or rejoiced in Judah's overthrow, Ammon, Moab, Edom, Philistia, Tyre, Zidon and Egypt. These prophecies are dated, like the others, and appeared at intervals during these two years. At length, the message for which Ezekiel had been waiting arrived, and with it came an entire change in the prophet's program. "In the twelfth year of our captivity, in the tenth month, in the fifth day of the month, one that had escaped out of Jerusalem came unto me saying, The city is smitten" (33:21). The news caused the greatest consternation among the exiles. Hitherto they had been so confident of a speedy termination to their expatriation that the words of Ezekiel had fallen upon deaf ears. Now all was changed. He was vindicated, and his influence immeasurably extended (33:30). But the sad news that Jerusalem was no more, and that the best and most resourceful of her people were on their way to Babylon in the company of their childless and blinded king, filled all hearts with a sense of utter depression and hopelessness. Clearly there was no future for Judah. No thought of return could now be cherished. The dream was past, the vision ended. Here then began the active work of Ezekiel once more. He was no longer dumb (33:22). It was necessary to restore confidence in the certainty of Jehovah's promises of restoration. To this object the messages of the third section of the book are devoted.

5. In these chapters (33-48) there is first set forth the responsibility of a shepherd of the people, a religious teacher; and the false shepherds, the professional prophets, are denounced as selfish and certain to be displaced (chapters 33, 34). Then the future program of the nation is presented in three aspects. First, the land of Judah, now defiled and possessed by enemies, especially the hated Edomites, is to be cleansed of their presence, and to become once more fruitful and inhabited, with cities walled and strong; and thus its reproach shall be removed (35; 36:1-15). But next, in order that the land may be inhabited by a pure people, the nation must be cleansed. This Jehovah will do, not because the people have merited it; but because His honor is at stake, and demands that His land shall be peopled by a nation worthy of His name. Therefore, he will sprinkle upon them the water of purgation (Num. 19:9-19), and give them a heart of flesh instead of their heart of stone. Moral renewal was an essential part of that future career of blessedness (36:16-38). In answer to the popular discouragement, in which the people compared themselves to dry bones, came the vision of the great

awakening of the nation (chapter 37), and the assurance was added that when in any future time the hordes of their enemies came pouring into the holy land, the Gogs and Magogs of barbarous regions, they should be utterly cut off by the divine power; their dead should require seven months for burial, and their weapons seven years for burning (chapters 38, 39). Lastly, in the purged land, there was to be erected a new temple, greater and more beautiful than the gorgeous sanctuary set up by Solomon, and made the center of a worship more elaborate by far than any hitherto known (chapters 40-48). In a vision Ezekiel beheld this fair fabric, while a heavenly guide with a measuring rod led him here and there, describing the various features of the sacred house, and the location of the tribes in the revived state. From this house there issued a river of pure water which sweetened and made fruitful all the barren region to the east and even freshened the waters of the Dead Sea. This vision Ezekiel presented to the people in Babylon, hanging, so to speak, a picture of the coming temple before their eyes; thereby kindling anew their hope and at the same time suggesting additional features of Levitical service whereby the people might become possessed of a new ideal of ceremonial holiness. Ezekiel saw as no prophet before him the necessity of securing a condition of seclusion and holiness in order that Israel should be honored and prosperous. Already the influences were

Ezekiel, the Shepherd of the Exiles

at work whereby the Jews were transformed from a nation into a church.

THE BOOK OF EZEKIEL

I. From the prophet's call to the siege of Jerusalem, chaps. 1-24.
  1. The call and commission of Ezekiel, chaps. 1-3. 2. Symbolic illustrations of the fall of Jerusalem, chaps. 4-7. 3. The sins of Jerusalem, and the departure of the divine glory therefrom, chaps. 8-11. 4. More of Ezekiel's sign language, chap. 12. 5. Denunciation of false prophets, chap. 13. 6. The inevitable result of sin, chap. 14. 7. A group of parables, chaps. 15-17. 8. Ezekiel's doctrine of individual responsibility, chap. 18. 9. Another group of parables, chap. 19. 10. A message to the elders, chap. 20. 11. The sin and fate of Jerusalem, chaps. 21-22. 12. Parable of the sisters, Israel and Judah, chap. 23. 13. The beginning of the siege, chap. 24.
II. An interval in the ministry of Ezekiel, while the siege of Jerusalem is in progress. Prophecies against Ammon, Moab, Edom, Philistia, Tyre, Zidon and Egypt, chaps. 25-32.
III. The period after the fall of Jerusalem, chaps. 33-48.
  1. The duty of the shepherd of souls, chaps. 33, 34. (The messenger with news of the destruction of the city, vs. 21, 22.) 2. The land of Judah to be cleansed of enemies, especially Edomites, and restored to fruitfulness and prosperity, 35: 1—36: 15. 3. The nation to be restored, purified and protected, 36: 16—39: 29. 4. The ideal sanctuary and its appointments, chaps. 40-48.

QUESTIONS

1. How long did the exile continue? How did the exiles live? What religious services were carried on? What dangers did Ezekiel seek to prevent? 2. What is known of this prophet? What was the significance

of his call? What truth did he emphasize? What signs did he use? What parables did he utter? 3. How do the writings of Ezekiel differ from those of Isaiah and Jeremiah? What events were transpiring at Jerusalem of which he was aware? What great doctrine did he set forth? 4. What nations are denounced in the second part of the book, and for what sins? Who brought word of the fall of Jerusalem? What was the effect? 5. What did Ezekiel now seek to do? What three things did he prophesy for the future? What was the purpose of the vision of a new temple?

CHAPTER XII

THE EVANGELICAL PROPHECY

1. The formal period of exile came to its close with the overthrow of the empire of Babylonia, and the advent of Cyrus of Persia as a world-ruler in 538 B. C. Long before this time, however, Ezekiel's work had closed, and new messages were needed in order to prepare and encourage the people to take advantage of the opportunity for return to Jerusalem when it should come. There was great danger that the long delay would result in a total loss of the expectation or desire to return. The whole providential mission of Israel was bound up with this restoration of the nation to its ancient home and the reconstruction of its temple and service. It was the task of the prophets to keep alive this hope, and one of the messages, the only one indeed which has been preserved to us, is recorded in the closing chapters of the book of Isaiah. The greater part of chapters 1-39 has been considered in an earlier section of this book (chapter 7). The fact that the section beginning with chapter 40 deals with the closing years of the exile constitutes the reason for its consideration at this point. The authorship of these chapters is an open question. Their position as a part of the book bearing the name

Isaiah is valuable evidence that they are the work of that prophet, or were thought to have been by those who arranged the book in its present form. Those who hold to the unity of the book affirm that these chapters, dealing as they clearly do with the exile, a period more than a century and a half after the close of Isaiah's ministry, were written by him in a prophetic ecstasy, by which he was transported in spirit into the later period and spoke out of that future situation to the people in Babylon. Many Bible scholars, however, regard these chapters as the words of some prophet living in the land of exile and in its closing years, whose endeavor it was to encourage his countrymen with the promise of divine mercy and assistance. Such a prophet would write rather than preach, and the danger of speaking openly the sentiments of this portion of the book would account, it is claimed, for the fact that the writer concealed his identity. The question of authorship is, however, far less important than the character of the message, and upon that point there is no ground for doubt. The power and beauty of these utterances, the high spiritual level on which, for the most part, they move, vindicates their right to a place in the very foremost rank of prophecy, while their Messianic character makes them almost an Old Testament gospel. For this reason the second section of the book has not infrequently nor inappropriately been called "The Evangelical Prophecy," the message

The Evangelical Prophecy 117

of good tidings to the exiles, the fair vision of Zion redeemed.

2. The prophecy opens with the majestic and yet tender words of consolation which have grown precious to Christians of succeeding ages, "Comfort ye, comfort ye, my people, saith your God" (40:1). In the fullness of that outflowing mercy the divine wrath is forgotten. The sins of the nation which made exile necessary are more than pardoned. A chorus of voices proclaims the approach of the crisis which shall usher in the new national life—a highway is to be prepared across the desert from Babylon to Jerusalem on which the returning pilgrims shall be led back to Zion (cf. chapter 35). To the sad lament of the nation that there are no longer leaders, but that all, like grass, have perished, the answer comes, "The grass, indeed, withers, the flower fades; but the word of our God shall stand forever" (vs. 6-8). Word is then sent to the cities of Judah announcing that God is about to lead back His people to reoccupy the waste places, and the prophet follows this with a magnificent statement of the power of Jehovah the God of Israel as contrasted with the poor creatures which Babylonian hands fashion into gods, and to which Babylonian knees are accustomed to bow (vs. 18-21). Both here and in 44:9-17 the tendency to be led away into idolatry, which beset many of the Jews, evokes the withering sarcasm of the writer as he describes the laborious process by which one of these gods

is gotten into form. In comparison with such vanities the Jew has a God whose majesty might well fill the heart of His worshipers with profound pride and satisfaction. And if the discouraged people were inclined to believe that their God had forgotten or was weary of them, he answers confidently, "Hast thou not known? Hast thou not heard? The everlasting God, Jehovah, the Creator of the ends of the earth, fainteth not, neither is weary. . . . He giveth power to the faint; and to him that hath no might He increaseth strength. Even the youths shall faint and be weary, and the young men shall utterly fall; but they that wait upon Jehovah shall renew their strength; they shall mount up with wings as eagles; they shall run and not be weary; they shall walk and not faint" (vs. 28-31). Such words were addressed to that type of thought so prevalent in Ezekiel's time, which regarded the fall of the nation as the result of Jehovah's inability to preserve it; and their lot in Babylon as a proof of the limitation of His power to the territory of Judah. As a consequence men grew skeptical of the value of faithfulness to their covenant God, and certain that there was no future for the nation. The prophet attempts to reanimate confidence by justifying the strange events of the past, but more by asserting the present power of God as universal Ruler. He alone can foresee the future and fashion the events of history to fulfill His purposes. What Babylonian god could do this (41:21-29)?

3. But God realizes His purposes not alone by direct interference with the movements of history, but as well, and most frequently, by the use of special instruments. It was a part of the prophetic work to proclaim a philosophy of history which recognized in the nations and their rulers the servants of Jehovah, who bring to pass, unconsciously perhaps, His great designs. Of this the prophet here is a special witness. At the period to which this prophecy belongs, Cyrus of Persia was moving on the northern and eastern frontier of the empire, but no amount of political sagacity or prescience was able to foresee his conquest of the city and his instrumentality in forwarding the providential ministry of Judah. Least of all was Cyrus conscious of any other motive than the desire to possess the throne of Babylon, now tottering to its fall. Yet the prophet repeatedly asserts that Cyrus is the servant of Jehovah, who is carrying forward His purposes. The first reference to him is made in connection with the claim that God can foresee and foretell the future. None of the gods of Babylon have known of it, yet the Holy One is raising up one from the north and east who shall overthrow rulers and bring down their gods (41:25). Among the many predictions of the restoration of Jerusalem there is one identifying Cyrus directly with its accomplishment (44:28; 45:1f.). Here he is called God's shepherd, to peform all His pleasure; His anointed (Messiah), whose right hand He

holds. Again, the prophet, speaking for God, asserts that this "ravenous bird from the east" is the man of Jehovah's counsel from a far country (46:11). Little did Cyrus appreciate the importance of his work in its effect upon the future, and the fact that the chief ground of his conspicuous place in history was to be his relation to an oppressed and obscure people in Babylonia, of whose religion and history he was all but totally ignorant. Thus, God uses unconscious and even hostile instruments to bring things to pass, and of these one of the most conspicuous examples is Cyrus the Great. The confidence with which the prophet declares the mission of Cyrus as a liberator of the Jews affords one of the most interesting instances of prediction contained in the Old Testament.

4. But the great idea which runs through these chapters and conditions all the prophet's thought regarding Israel and the future is that of the Servant of Jehovah. In the first part of the book of Isaiah the conception of the Messianic King is prominent. Here it does not occur, but its place is taken by the picture of a ministry of self-devotion and suffering which is to eventuate in perfect success, and be the means not only of saving the nation, but the world. There is marked progress also in the prophet's thought regarding the Servant. At first the whole nation is regarded as the specially chosen messenger to perform the divine will, selected in the distant past, and now passing

through a period of discipline to further fit him for his work. With such a broad, national conception of the personality of the Servant the prophet, speaking for God, says, "But thou, Israel, my Servant, Jacob, whom I have chosen, the seed of Abraham my friend, . . . fear thou not" (41:8, 9). Pursuing the same theme, and contemplating not only the mission of the Servant, but the quiet, undemonstrative methods by which he was to accomplish his work, the prophet says, "Behold my Servant, whom I uphold; my chosen, in whom my soul delighteth; I have put my spirit upon him; he shall bring forth judgment to the nations. He shall not cry, nor lift up, nor cause his voice to be heard in the street; a bruised reed shall he not break, and the smoking flax shall he not quench; he shall bring forth judgment in truth" (42:1-3). Here it is the nation as a whole which is regarded as empowered to bring to consummation the divine purpose. But the nation is far from perfect; its sin and blindness to truth have all but disqualified it to perform so lofty a service. "Hear, ye deaf," says the prophet, "look, ye blind, that ye may see. Who is blind, but my Servant, and deaf as my messenger, that I send" (42:18, 19)? Nevertheless, the nation is encouraged to undertake its great task; "Fear not, for I have redeemed thee; I have called thee by thy name; thou art mine" (43:1); "Ye are my witnesses, saith the Lord, and my Servant whom I have chosen" (v. 10); "Fear not,

O Jacob, my Servant; and thou, Jeshuran, whom I have chosen" (44:2). Speaking of the nothingness of idols, he says, "Remember these things, O Jacob; and Israel, for thou art my Servant" (44:21), and to Cyrus he cries, "For Jacob my Servant's sake, and Israel my chosen I have called thee by thy name" (45:4). In all these passages the identification of the Servant as the whole nation now passing through affliction, but about to emerge into a new life of power, is clear. Jehovah has no other means of accomplishing His gracious purposes in the world than the people whom He has for centuries been training for this task. They are a redemptive race, a nation on whose future the spiritual prospects of the world depend, the seed of Abraham, through whom all nations shall be blessed. Hence, the importance of the revival of the national life at Jerusalem, which is the great object of the prophet's message. This is the thought which pervades the first section of this prophecy (chapters 40-48).

5. But in the second section, which opens with chapter 49, there is a change in the thought of the prophet regarding the Servant. Already he is conscious of the weakness and imperfection of the nation as a whole. Many Jews have become apostates, and others are maintaining their faith with difficulty. A comparatively small portion of the people is really prepared to undertake so important a task as that which Jehovah has committed to Israel. This is the rem-

nant of which earlier prophets had spoken, the righteous seed that gives promise of the new nation. To this remnant, this faithful portion of the people, the prophetic conception of the Servant now narrows itself, gaining at the same time new intensity and significance in the process. The mission set before this messenger is the double task of saving the unfaithful Israelites and the outside world. Gradually this idea emerges from the former. Personifying the Servant, the prophet puts into his mouth these words: "The Lord hath called me from the womb; . . . He hath made me a polished shaft; . . . and He said unto me, Thou art my Servant; Israel in whom I will be glorified. And now saith the Lord that formed me to be His Servant, to bring Jacob again to Him, It is too light a thing that thou shouldest be my Servant to raise up the tribes of Jacob, and to restore the preserved of Israel: I will also give thee for a light to the Gentiles" (49:5, 6). Here the distinction between the entire nation and the righteous remnant is clearly marked. But even this remnant was unable to perform the great task, and still another phase of the theme finds expression in the prophet's words. One greater than nation or remnant must appear to complete the ministry for which neither of these was sufficient, and the third figure appears, that of the Messianic Servant, the embodiment of all the elements which resided in the nation and the remnant, save sin. He at last is able to accomplish the mighty task.

Professor Delitzsch thus describes the conception which is developed in this prophecy: "The idea of the Servant of Jehovah, assumed, as it were, the form of a pyramid; the base was the people of Israel as a whole, the central section was Israel according to the Spirit, and the apex is the person of the mediator of salvation springing out of Israel. And the last of the three is regarded (1) as the center of the circle of the promised kingdom—the second David; (2) the center of the circle of the people of salvation—the second Israel; (3) the center of the circle of the human race—the second Adam." This is the thought which pervades the section 52:13—53:12, which is justly esteemed the gem of all prophecy. It describes the success of the Servant's mission in spite of misunderstanding and suffering. Its five paragraphs set forth the successive steps of His redemptive work, and voice the feelings of one who from outside beheld, at first with skepticism, then astonishment, and at last reverence, the ministry of the suffering Servant of God. While these utterances refer primarily to the righteous part of the nation, as the uncomplaining saints whose martyr deaths like that of Jeremiah emphasized the redemptive character of their afflictions, yet they find their full significance only in the life and death of One greater than all prophets and martyrs of Israel, "who for the joy that was set before Him endured the cross, despising shame, and hath sat down at the right hand of the throne of God" (Heb. 12:2). Here the Messianic hope finds its fullest expression. The later chapters of this prophecy present other features of the Servant's work and the happy future whose blessings are mediated by His ministry. Some portions of the material have been thought to refer to still subsequent periods of the history, during the depressing years in which Jerusalem was slowly reviving. But there are no more inspiring notes in all prophetic writings than are struck in the great missionary chapters of this book (55, 60) which proclaim the universal purpose of the message of God, and the statement of the work of the Servant and the program of the coming age (61), upon which Jesus laid His hand one day in the synagogue at Nazareth, saying, "To-day hath this Scripture been fulfilled in your ears" (Luke 4:21).

ISAIAH, 40-66.

I. The certainty of the coming deliverance, Isa. 40-48.
1. The prophetic voices; comfort, preparation, return, the power of God, 40. 2. Israel the Servant of Jehovah; idols challenged, 41. 3. The quiet methods of the Servant; the passion of Jehovah; the Servant's weakness, 42. 4. Israel, the Servant, precious to Jehovah, though unworthy, 43. 5. Israel shall again be prosperous; idols are nothing; Jerusalem shall be rebuilt; Cyrus is coming, 44. 6. Cyrus divinely used for Israel; futility of withstanding God, 45. 7. Idols of Babylon to be carried away as spoil when Cyrus comes, 46. 8. Babylon shall be humiliated, 47. 9. God, who knows the future, will save Israel, for His name's sake. Go forth from Babylon, 48.

II. The mission of the Servant, 49-57.
1. The Servant, now the remnant, is to redeem the nation and the world, 49. 2. The Servant, having suffered, can help others, 50. 3. Trust in God; awake to new life; you shall no more be afflicted; announce the return to Jerusalem, 51: 1—52: 12. 4. The Servant's success in his mission, 52: 13—53: 12. The Servant shall prosper (13-15); we thought he suffered for his own sins (1-3); but he suffered for us (4-6); he was submissive to his hard fate (7-9); there was a divine plan in it all, and complete success is the result (10-12). 5. The happy prospect of the people, 54. 6. The universal invitation; certainty of redemption, and the widening of its circle, 55: 1—56: 8. 7. Indignation against false prophets and the disloyal portion of Israel, 56: 9—57: 21.

III. Zion restored; the servants and the sinners, 58-66.
1. Jehovah desires true righteousness, not formal service, 58. 2. Redemption is hindered by the sins of the people, 59. 3. Vision of the nation restored to Zion in prosperity and glory, 60. 4. The program of the new age, 61. 5. Zion must be fully restored; prepare for the return, 62. 6. The divine warrior from Edom, 63: 1-6. 7. Prophet's appeal to God in behalf of the prostrate nation, 63: 7—64: 12. 8. God is more than ready, but the nation has refused help; the servants of God shall be blessed; the disobedient shall be destroyed, 65, 66.

QUESTIONS

1. What was the task of the prophets during the exile? What are the two views regarding the authorship of Isaiah 40-66? What is the character of the work as compared with other prophecies? Why is it called "the evangelical prophecy"? 2. What is its opening message? What highway is to be constructed? What is said of the gods of Babylon? How were the Jews tempted to regard Jehovah?

The Evangelical Prophecy

3. Whom had God chosen for His servant at the time? What were Cyrus' motives? What light do these predictions throw on the prophetic power to foresee? 4. What is the great idea of this prophecy? What progress marks the conception of the Servant? Who is the Servant first understood to be? 5. How is this thought narrowed in the next section? Who is the Servant here? What is his task? How does Professor Delitzsch describe the Servant passages? What is the gem of prophecy? What special chapters later in the section?

CHAPTER XIII

HAGGAI AND ZECHARIAH, THE PROPHETS OF THE REVIVAL OF JERUSALEM

1. The decree of Cyrus in 538 B. C. permitted the return of such Jews as desired to go to Jerusalem. The number of Jews who actually started for Jerusalem under Sheshbazzar was, however, probably small. The census recorded in Ezra, chapter 2, is evidently a register of those who were residents in the province of Judah at a period several years later. There were probably very few who came at first, and their numbers were increased but slowly by subsequent arrivals. The people who remained in the land, the "remnant," as the prophets Haggai and Zechariah called them, were still the most considerable portion of the community as late as 520 B. C. It was more than fifteen years after the edict of Cyrus had been proclaimed and the earliest attempts at return had been made under Sheshbazzar, that these prophets undertook to promote the building of the temple, whose foundations had been begun in the second year, after the arrival of the first caravan (Ezra 3). During all that time nothing had been done toward the completion of the undertaking. The people were disinclined to take up the task of building the temple, both because they were poor and because there were troubles

for the community arising from the antagonism of the people who inhabited the surrounding territory. The prospect was sufficiently disheartening when Haggai and Zechariah began their work.

2. At last, however, Haggai, in the year 520 B. C., in the month of September, undertook to stir up the people to a sense of their responsibility to God. They were commonly saying that the time had not yet come to build the temple (Haggai 1:2), but, on the other hand, they were living in frame houses. The prophet undertook to show them that their complaints arose from causes that lay in their power to remedy. They had been troubled recently by drought and famine (1:6, 10, 11). The prophet assured them that it was because of their failure to fulfill the wishes of God by rebuilding His house that they had thus suffered, and he exhorted them to go up to the mountain and to bring timber that the house might be finished (1:8). The effect of this sermon was immediate. The leaders of the people, Zerubbabel and Joshua, undertook the work, and a beginning was made in the building operations some twenty-five days later in the month. In October of the same year the prophet appeared with a new message, which seemed to be called forth by a partial abandonment of the enterprise, resulting perhaps from discouragement or weariness on the part of the builders. There were those in the community who were reporting that, having seen the old temple in the days

before it was destroyed, they were vastly disappointed at the meagerness of the new structure which was rising. Such words produced a feeling of indifference and discouragement on the part of the community at large. The prophet, therefore, rose to meet the emergency with a new message. Jehovah had covenanted with the people when they came out of Egypt that He would be with them. That covenant still held good. They might expect the aid of Jehovah if they fulfilled His wishes. Moreover, all the signs of the times pointed to great political changes in the empire. It was the moment when the throne left by Cyrus to Cyaxares, his son, and later occupied by the usurper Gomates (Gaumata), had just been occupied by Darius, who was elected by the princes to the kingship. This election was the signal for revolts in many provinces, and a state so feeble as Judah might well believe that where universal peace promised only continuance of meager and unpromising conditions, a general upheaval of the empire would bring a measure of prosperity to the little state. The prophet, therefore, predicts such convulsions in the empire as will bring the riches of the nations into Jerusalem (2:6, 7).

3. Contemporary with Haggai (Ezra 5:1), and probably somewhat younger, was Zechariah, a man of priestly family (Neh. 12:4, 16), unlike his colleague, who was a layman (Hag. 2:11). It was his task to assist in the enterprise of getting the temple

built. The book which is called by his name has been thought by Bible students to contain some materials which date from other periods than that of the prophet himself, but that the first eight chapters are the authentic work of Zechariah there is no question, and through these chapters we are able to understand the problems which confronted the prophets in this period and see the difficulties with which they had to contend in the task of securing the gradual revival of national life in Judah. The character of these writings of Zechariah is somewhat peculiar in several respects. They deal largely in visions. This characteristic finds small place in the work of such great prophets as Amos, Hosea, Isaiah, Micah and Jeremiah; but in the later periods of prophecy, in what we may call the declining era, visions and other similar elements reappear in prophecy. Another characteristic is the apocalyptic symbolism which enters into the visions. Here are seen the striking figures which appear so frequently in the apocalypses both of the Old and New Testaments. A third feature is seen in the large element of angelic mediation between God and man. The prophet no longer seems to stand in the closest intimacy with God, but is instructed by an angel, who acts as his spiritual interpreter and guide; and many of the actions of the visions are carried forward by angels, representing either human or divine forces, whose workings affect more or less the destiny of Judah. It must not, however, be supposed, because the prophecies of the later period move upon a lower level and seem to have lost something of the power and directness of the earlier messages of God, that they are, therefore, valueless, or to be lightly disregarded. The whole condition of affairs in the post-exilic period was discouraging to a degree, and if prophetic activity shared somewhat the depressing influence of Judah's environment, it should not be regarded as strange.

4. The prophet Zechariah appeared, so far as we have record, first in November of the year 520 B. C., just about the time Darius was consolidating his turbulent empire and seating himself firmly upon its throne. The introduction to the book is found in 1:1-6, in an oracle which emphasizes the abiding certainty of the utterances of God. Again, in January of the year 519 B. C., Zechariah appeared with a new message, embracing a series of visions which he had seen and which bore encouraging messages to the people of Jerusalem. These eight visions, which apparently were seen by the prophet in one night, are contained in the section 1:7—6:8, and deal with the following particulars: Four horsemen who have patrolled the earth report that there is universal quiet, which from the standpoint of Judah, desirous as it was of the overturning of the empire in order that it might be profited thereby, seemed sufficiently unpromising; but to the indignant protest of the angel of God there came the divine answer of comfort in the

assurance that God was jealous for Jerusalem and would surely return to help her. In the second vision four horns, which in apocalyptic symbolism stand for political powers or kings, are beaten down by four workmen armed with hammers, indicating the downfall of those nations, under whose oppressive tyranny Judah had suffered. The third vision discloses a man, who, as the sequel shows, is an angel, with a measuring line in his hand, going forth to measure Jerusalem for a new set of walls, but he is assured that walls are unnecessary and impracticable, both because the city will be too populous to be enclosed within walls and because Jehovah will Himself be her protection. Verses 6-13 contain an exhortation to the exiles still in Babylon to escape to Judah during the favorable interval of political unrest. In the fourth vision the general poverty and misery of the community are described in symbolic terms. Joshua, the priestly representative of the nation, is described as clothed in filthy garments and accused by the satan; but the priest is justified by the divine voice and clothed with rich apparel, while the Messianic promises are given to the people. In the fifth vision the prophet saw a golden candlestick, with seven lamps, supplied with olive oil through pipes connecting them with two olive trees. The explanation of the vision is interrupted by an oracle to Zerubbabel (Zech. 4:6b—10a), which seems to belong after verse 14. The candlestick stood for the restored sanctuary; the lamps for the divine presence; and the olive trees for the two anointed ones ("sons of oil") of the community, Zerubbabel the prince and Joshua the priest, the supporters of the new commonwealth. The prophet's purpose to emphasize the importance of these two men to the city and the temple is apparent. The second part of the vision is the message to Zerubbabel, as the chief pillar of the new state. The sixth vision is that of the flying roll, with its curses on stealing and perjury. In the seventh vision the same thought is pursued. The temptation to false weights and measures was prevalent among a people environed, as were the Jews, in this period, with the mercantile spirit, but afflicted still with poverty. The temptation is, therefore, described as a woman thrust into a measure and held down with a weight, which is then carried far away to Babylon, the land of all iniquity, where it is left. In the last vision the thought returns once more to the broader political horizon, and the chariots of the four winds are described as patrolling the earth to bring word regarding the divine enterprise among the nations. Some recent report of political uprising seems to be referred to in this message. The next section of the book describes the receipt of gifts of gold and silver from Jews in Babylon, out of which a crown was made for the leader of the state (6:9-15). Then follows the question regarding fasts, and the prophet's response (7:1-7); the statement of warnings

Haggai and Zechariah

sent to earlier generations (vs. 8-14), and several short messages relating to the return of Jehovah to Jerusalem, the growth of population, the blessing to be expected, and the future honor of the Jews (8:1-23). The remaining chapters of the book apparently deal with quite other situations, unrelated to Zechariah's time; but among their utterances are found the description of the Messianic King's advent into His capital (9:9, 10; cf. Matt. 21:4, 5); the symbolic message regarding the rejected shepherd (chapter 11), and the apocalyptic description of the battle of the nations against Jerusalem (chapter 14).

THE BOOK OF HAGGAI

1. First discourse (Sept., 520 B. C.), insisting upon immediate efforts to build the temple, 1: 1-11. 2. The work begun by the people, 1: 12-15. 3. Second discourse (Oct., 520 B. C.), encouraging the people, who had abandoned the work, 2: 1-9. 4. Third discourse (Dec., 520 B. C.), regarding the ceremonial uncleanness of the nation, 2: 10-19. 5. Fourth discourse, the same day; promises of political prosperity, 2: 20-23.

THE BOOK OF ZECHARIAH

I. The abiding word of God (Nov., 520 B. C.), 1: 1-6.
II. Eight night-visions of Zechariah (Jan., 519 B. C.), 1: 7—6: 8.
   1. The four horsemen, 1: 7-17. 2. The four horns and the four smiths, 1: 8-21. 3. The man with the measuring line, 2: 1-5. [An inserted song: a promise of deliverance, 2: 6-13.] 4. The high priest Joshua and the satan; the Messianic hope, 3: 1-10. 5. The

seven-branched lamp, and the two olive trees, 4: 1-14. 6. The flying roll; thieves and perjurers banished, 5: 1-4. 7. The woman in the measure, 5:5-11. 8. The chariots of the four winds, 6: 1-8.
III. The crown for the prince of Judah; the political hopes of the people, 6: 1-8.
IV. The question regarding fasts; the prophet's answer, 7: 17 (Dec., 518 B. C.).
V. Unheeded warnings sent to earlier generations through the prophets; their rejection and the result, 7: 8-14.
VI. Short oracles on various themes, 8: 1-3. 1. Jehovah's return to Jerusalem, 8: 1-3. 2. People of all ages shall dwell in Jerusalem, 8: 4-6. 3. Exiles to return, 8: 7, 8. 4. Curses changed to blessings on condition of righteousness, 8: 9-17. 5. Fasts to be changed to joy, 8-18, 19. 6. Nations shall seek Zion; the Jew honored, 8: 20-23.
VII. The remaining chapters of the book, 9-14.

QUESTIONS

1. When did the formal period of the exile end? What was the character of the earliest return to Judah? How did the work of temple building progress? What two prophets encouraged this work? 2. What attitude of the people did the sermons of Haggai endeavor to meet and correct? What facts hindered the building of the temple? What was his success? What caused the work to cease? What expectations filled the hearts of the Jews? 3. How was the work of Zechariah related to that of Haggai? What is the character of his writings? How do the prophecies of this period compare with those of earlier times. 4. What is the general outline of the prophecy? What eight visions constitute its leading feature? What is their meaning? What may be said of the remaining chapters of the book?

CHAPTER XIV

LATER PROPHETIC BOOKS — MALACHI, JOEL, JONAH AND DANIEL

1. The reign of Darius I. (521-485 B. C.), who had only just secured his throne in the times of Haggai and Zechariah, was followed by that of Xerxes I. (485-464 B. C.), the Ahasuerus of the book of Esther. During this long period there was little, if any, change in the condition of Jerusalem. The aspirations of the Jews for political power led apparently to the quiet suppression of the royal line of David by the Persian authorities and the substitution of a non-Jewish governor for the native prince. The temple had been completed in 516 B. C., but the walls of Jerusalem lay in ruins as they were left by the departing armies of Nebuchadrezzar in 586 B. C. Probably companies of Jews arrived from the east from time to time, but the condition of affairs was not encouraging, and the people were far from enthusiastic regarding the temple service. This is the situation revealed by the book of Malachi, which seems to belong late in this period, probably shortly before the reformatory movements instituted by Nehemiah and Ezra, or perhaps in the interval between the first and second residences of the former in Judah. The prophecy appears to be anonymous, as "Malachi" can hardly be taken as

a proper name; it means "my messenger," and was probably used as a title from the fact that it was one of the striking words employed in the book itself (cf. 3:1). The writer reproves both people and priests for conduct unbecoming a nation belonging to God. Polluted bread is offered at the sanctuary, and animals are presented as sacrificial victims that are blind, lame and sick. They would not have the effrontery to offer presents of this character to their Persian governor; how dare they so insult God (1:6-8, 13)? Far better shut the temple than so defile it (v. 10). Jehovah's name is held in reverence among the heathen; His own people should at least show Him equal honor (vs. 11, 14). The priests are especially rebuked for failing to conform to the example set by Levi their ancestor (2:1-9). Two other sins receive fitting denunciation, that of marrying wives from among the heathen (vs. 11, 12), and that of divorce (vs. 13-16). In such a condition of affairs the divine messenger may be expected to suddenly appear and with purifying chastisements purge priests and people (3:1f.). There was still time for repentance, however. Let the city turn to God and bring the tithes for the temple which they had neglected and they should yet be blessed (3:7f.). That there was a body of faithful men in Jerusalem is witnessed by the prophet's reference to their meetings for mutual help and encouragement (3:16, 17). But they were probably few in numbers as compared with the indifferent. The book closes with warnings to the latter to beware of the day of retribution to come, and with the promise that Elijah, the fearless reformer, shall come to set things right (chapter 4). Thus the Old Testament comes to an end with words of stern severity toward the scorners, but of warm commendation for the righteous who observe the law of Moses.

2. The book of Joel has been assigned by different Bible scholars to various periods in the history of the nation, but many indications make increasingly probable a date some time after the days of Ezra Of the prophet himself we know nothing beyond the fact that his father was named Pethuel. A plague of locusts furnishes the occasion for the work. The visitation is so severe that nothing can be recalled to compare with it. The crops have been stripped from the land; as a result a famine is afflicting the people to such an extent that even the meal offerings of the temple are lacking (1:1-13). In view of their terrible destitution the prophet calls for a solemn fast, and a public assembly (vs. 14-20). But he foresees that a greater danger is approaching—the day of Jehovah, a time of judgment. A mysterious enemy is to invade the city, whose coming will cause the stoutest heart to tremble. This unnamed foe will utterly waste the land (2:1-11). Still there is time for deliverance, if the people are sincere in their wish to escape the approaching doom; and once more the prophet calls for a solemn assem-

bly of the entire people, to pray that the doom may be averted (vs. 12-17). The second section describes the result of this gathering, which is supposed to have taken place. Jehovah is roused to assist His people. He promises instant relief; the locust plague shall be dispersed, the enemy shall be driven away, the land shall again be fruitful, and the divine power shall be vindicated. Then the greater blessing shall descend—a blessing for which all the rest was but a prelude; the Spirit of God shall be poured out upon all the nation, and in the midst of terrible signs those who survive the ordeal of purification shall enjoy the salvation promised (2:18-32). Chapter 3 reflects a situation far more favorable. The dangers before mentioned have passed away. In confidence, the prophet looks abroad, certain that the restoration of the Jews to their national life, now only partial, will be made complete, while the nations that have had to do with their spoliation shall feel the scourge of retribution. To these nations the prophet exultantly flings out a challenge to war. He sees them gather in the valley of Jehoshaphat only to be overthrown by Jehovah. Their lands shall henceforth be desolate, but Jerusalem shall be prosperous and protected. In this book are manifested a deep interest in the priestly elements of the religious life, an almost total absence of rebukes for sin, such as characterized the great prophets, a limitation of the field of divine favor and blessing to

Judah, and a feeling of hatred for other nations. But upon the deep interest of God in His people, and His willingness to deliver them, there is strong emphasis, while the splendid prophecy of the outpouring of the Spirit (2:28-32), the gem of the book, came to its true fulfillment amid the flaming signs of Pentecost (Acts 2:14-21).

(3) But if there were prophets who perceived only a part of the truth and, realizing God's providential care for the chosen people, failed to grasp the full significance of the national mission to the world, there were others who were able to comprehend a fuller measure of the divine purpose, and pointed out the narrowness of that type of Jewish thought which made the nation the exclusive object of God's regard, and the other nations only valueless aggregates of humanity, without other destiny than destruction. Both attitudes of mind were represented in the community, though the narrow and exclusive view rapidly gained ground after the return from exile, and came to its fullest expression in the Pharisaism of the days of Jesus. But if the advocates of the national and selfish view claimed the sanction of Ezekiel and still more of Joel, failing to discern their deeper spiritual qualities, they met the pronounced opposition of other prophets of the past and of their own day. The whole spirit of the evangelical prophecy was universal and missionary. In it Israel and the Messiah alike found their true service in the salvation of the world. Similar is

the tone of the book of Jonah, which in this respect stands in striking contrast with Joel. Many indications point to this period as the date of the book. The author recounts the missionary journey of Jonah, the son of Amittai, a native of Gathhepher, a town of Zebulon, who prophesied in the reign of Jeroboam II. (2 Kings 14:25). The narrative begins with his call to preach the coming doom of Nineveh, the hated capital of Assyria. But the prophet had no love for this heathen city, and preferred to let it perish. He, therefore, sought to escape his task by flight to the west. Stopped in his career by a storm, and restored to his own land by miraculous means, he no longer attempted to evade his mission, but proceeded to Nineveh. Here his proclamation of impending doom produced such an impression that the whole city repented, fasting and wearing sackcloth, even the beasts sharing these signs of penitence. As a result, the city was spared. But the prophet, whose ungracious and prejudiced spirit is apparently the object of the author's rebuke, was deeply angered at the display of divine mercy, and protested that he knew from the first that such was God's disposition, and so he had endeavored to evade his task. With tender words of reproof the hot and petulant man is reminded of the pity due from God to all His creatures, of whom so many were to be found in Nineveh. Thus the prophetic writer of a period when the later Judaism was already taking form,

Later Prophetic Books 143

sought to point out the unlovely attitude of many of his countrymen toward the world whose spiritual welfare had been entrusted to them; and in so doing made use of this narrative of the past. Few portions of Holy Scripture approach the book of Jonah in beauty, breadth of view, emphasis upon the necessity of repentance, and portrayal of the divine tenderness and love for all mankind. "The sign of the prophet Jonah" was used by Jesus with telling effect in reproof of the spirit of the people in His own day. The Jews would not listen to His preaching and demanded a sign, but He told them that a heathen nation had repented at the message of Jonah, and a greater than Jonah was there (Matt. 12:38-41; 16:4; Luke 11:29-32).

4. The book of Daniel was not placed by the Jews among the prophetic books, but with the miscellaneous writings of the Old Testament. This may have been owing to their feeling that it was not entitled to such a position, or to the accepted list of prophetic books being closed before it made its appearance. But in spite of the fact that it is unlike the prophetic books in many respects, and conforms more closely to the apocalyptic literature of later Judaism, it contains narratives of the greatest interest, and prophetic elements whose influence must have been profound in the period at which it was issued, and which have engaged the earnest thought of Christians in every generation. The situation to which the book addresses itself appears to have been the

days of persecution just preceding the outbreak of the Maccabean revolt from the tyranny of Antiochus Epiphanes, king of Syria (166 B. C.). The writer, to encourage his countrymen to resist the influences that were threatening to overthrow the last remnants of the faith, gathered up the narratives regarding Daniel, a Hebrew who rose to the highest honor in the court of Nebuchadrezzar of Babylon. His purpose was apparently to hold up before his despairing countrymen the examples of heroism handed down from a previous age, and to inspire them to new hope by prophecies of the early downfall of the tyrant, whom he describes under various symbols, as the little horn (7:8, 21; 8 9), the king of fierce countenance (8:23), the one that makes desolate (9:27), and the contemptible person (11:21f.). This destruction of their enemy was to be followed by the Messianic future of blessedness. The first section of the book (chapters 1 6) speaks of the experiences of Daniel and his three friends in Babylon, their self-restraint and heroism in face of the greatest dangers, as well as the eminent position which they, especially Daniel, obtained by interpreting the will of God. The second section (chapters 7-12) presents in the form of prediction and in apocalyptic symbols a picture of the world powers and the history of the period from Daniel's day to that of the Messianic period, expected soon after the author's own time. In this book the expectation of the future life shines out clearly, and the separation between the good and evil as a feature of the hereafter is a part of its teaching (12:2), while one of its most beautiful utterances is contained in the familiar passage: "They that be wise shall shine as the brightness of the firmament, and they that turn many to righteousness as the stars forever and ever" (12:3).

THE BOOK OF MALACHI

1. Polluted offerings presented at the temple, chap. 1. 2. The sins of the priests, 2:1-9. 3. Marriage of heathen women, and divorce, 2:10-17. 4. The coming messenger, 3:1-6. 5. The withholding of tithes, 3:7-12. 6. The disobedient and the pious, 3:13-18. 7. The day of the Lord, and the coming Elijah, chap. 4.

THE BOOK OF JOEL

I. Divine judgments, past and to come, 1:1—2:17.
1. The locust plague, 1:2-13. 2. Call for a fast in view of the terrible condition, 1:14-20. 3. Yet even a more dreadful enemy approaches, 2:1-11. 4. Turning to God may avail; a call to supplication, 2:12-17.
II. The divine response to the prophet's appeal, 2:18—3:21.
1. Jehovah aroused for His people's help, 2:18-27. 2. Outpouring of the Spirit; signs; deliverance, 2:28-32. 3. The prophet's challenge; the battle of nations; Zion victorious, chap. 3.

THE BOOK OF JONAH

1. The prophet's commission, flight, and rescue, 1:1-16. 2. The psalm of thanksgiving, 1:17—2:10. 3. Jonah at Nineveh, the repentance of the people, the prophet's anger and rebuke, 3:1—4:11.

THE BOOK OF DANIEL

I. Narratives of Hebrew heroism and wisdom, chaps. 1-6.
1. The four Hebrews at the court, chap. 1. 2. The king's vision of the image, and its interpretation, chap. 2. 3. The three Hebrews in the fiery furnace, chap. 3. 4. Nebuchadrezzar's humiliation, chap. 4. 5. Belshazzar's feast, chap. 5. 6. Daniel in the den of lions, chap. 6.
II. Visions of the kingdoms, chaps. 7-12.
1. The four beasts, the little horn, and the kingdom of saints, chap. 7. 2. The ram and the he-goat, chap. 8. 3. The seventy weeks, chap. 9. 4. The angel princes, the kings of Syria and Egypt, the oppressor, chaps. 10, 11. 5. Closing words of promise, chap. 12.

QUESTIONS

1. What was the character of the period succeeding the days of Haggai and Zechariah? What is known regarding the authorship of Malachi? What sins does it rebuke? What threatenings does it utter? 2. What was the occasion which called forth the book of Joel? What call is made in view of the danger? What great promise is voiced in this book? What is the attitude of the writer toward heathen nations? 3. What other disposition toward the heathen is manifested in the book of Jonah? What is known of this prophet? How did the author seek to rebuke the narrowness of his time? 4. What are the leading characteristics of the book of Daniel? To what situation does the book address itself? What is the character of the first half? Of the second? What is its teaching regarding the future life?

CHAPTER XV

THE MESSIANIC HOPE

1. Israel was a nation of hope and promise. Unlike other peoples, its Golden Age was in the future, not in the past. From the earliest beginning of national consciousness it was a gradually developing belief that Israel had a special mission, separate from the rest of the world, yet in some important degree connected with the spiritual life of the world. The divine purpose for humanity was believed to lie implicit in the unfolding history of this people. The Hebrew records preserved the first promise made to the race (Gen. 3:15), a promise that, though the struggle between good and evil should be long and bitter, yet in the end the good should triumph. This divine purpose manifested itself in the selection of certain individuals or tribes, through whose life the disclosure of the plans of God was to be made. But it was not a selection for favor, but rather for service. Israel was the chosen people of God, but not for its own sake. It had a ministry for the world. Its leaders were prophets, priests and kings, and these men, especially the prophets, were unique in their character and work. Their counterpart is not to be found in any other history. But in the last analysis the nation as a whole was regarded as royal, as priestly,

as prophetic (Ex. 19:6). What these special men did as leaders for the nation, Israel as a unit was to do for the world. Herein lay its unique office. But from the time of Amos and Hosea it was seen that the nation as a whole was unprepared for such a ministry. The religion of Jehovah was set aside too often for that of other gods, or was mixed with unworthy elements that robbed it of its effectiveness. A cleansing process alone could purify the people and make them worthy of their high ministry; and the agency through which this regeneration was to be wrought was recognized by all the prophets of that period as being national overthrow by Assyria, and later Babylonia. Only such a purification as should come through disaster and suffering could avail to prepare Israel for its true mission. But after this period of suffering had passed, the "remnant" or survivors would be worthy and a glorious future should be expected.

2. That future was to be the Messianic age, holy and marked by the presence of God. The consecration of kings and priests was signified by their anointing with the holy oil. From this word "anointed" or "Messiah," grew up the idea of the future glorious time as "anointed" or "Messianic." The conception of a person, who should stand as the common denominator of the new period of national salvation and purification, is first presented by Isaiah. In his rebuke of king Ahaz for presumptuous disregard of God, the prophet announces the birth of a

child, in whose day, soon to dawn (Isa. 7:14), and under whose leadership as a conqueror, and yet a prince of peace (Isa. 9:6, 7), the national deliverance was to be achieved; after which there would come the period of happiness and peace (Isa. 11:18). That Isaiah expected this child-king of the house of David in his own day seems certain; and herein is disclosed one of the interesting factors of prophecy. The outlines of the coming order of things were apparent to the eyes of the prophet, but the hour of the arrival was not so clear. The drama of redemption was contracted into a single scene, but its larger meaning lay implicit in the slowly unfolding movements upon which they looked. Deliverance from Assyria came, but not through the rise at that time of the Messianic king. Yet the vision was true, for the larger outlines of the Messianic time yet ahead fitted in no small degree the local distress and the certainly unforeseen deliverance. It remained for a later prophetic utterance to set forth a yet clearer vision of the true character of the Messianic work and the outlines of the Messianic figure. The Evangelical Prophecy discloses the Messianic hope in its fullest light, and does this under the figure of the suffering Servant of God. Here at first Israel as a whole is the Servant (Isa. 41:8; 44:1f.). Though fallen upon unhappy days, yet this very time is one of purification; and now that the process of purgation is reaching its completion, it is time to prepare for larger things to come. Redemption is not to be wrought by war and strife, as was the earlier view, but by peaceful methods (Isa. 42:1-4), and therefore, the figure of the king no longer appears, but the Servant in a humble and yet successful work. Presently, however, the idea that the nation as a whole can do the great work appears to be abandoned. Too many are indifferent. The remnant, the best part of the nation, is all that can be counted upon in such an enterprise. This remnant will save not only the apostate part of the nation, but the world at large (Isa. 49:5-7). But even the remnant was weak and unable to accomplish the divine work; and at last One rises from the remnant, a representative of both it and the whole nation, able to do that which both had failed to accomplish, the divine Servant, the Messiah. In Isaiah 52:13—53:12 the success of the Servant's mission is set forth in terms that show the blending of the personal and the national ideas about the Messianic figure. That this conception of the Messiah finds its fulfillment in the historic work of Jesus Christ is the teaching of the New Testament.

3. Messianic prophecy is not, therefore, a collection of texts taken from various books of the Old Testament and describing the personal life of Jesus. It is indeed frequently said by the New Testament writers that certain statements, which apparently have a local meaning for the past period in which they were written, were fulfilled in

the life of Christ. This usage is to be explained by recognition of the fact that the connection between Old Testament events and the life of Christ was seen to be very intimate, for He, as the Servant of Jehovah, took up the task which Israel could not accomplish, and thus many incidents or utterances that in their time had possessed only a local and temporary interest were seen to coincide with episodes in the life of the Messiah, in whom all the past found its new expression. So they came to have a new significance, *i. e.*, to be "fulfilled" in Him. But it is not in this list of passages that the true Messianic prophecy is to be found. It moves upon a much higher plane. There are, indeed, predictions, direct and specific, regarding the personality and surroundings of the Christ, but these predictions even if less numerous than sometimes supposed, rather gain than lose in value by this fact. Thus the Messianic hope is seen to have had its rise out of national distress. As long as Israel prospered it was in no need of other stimulus. But when trouble came, the mind of the nation, under the inspiring promises of prophets, turned to the future, and expected deliverance in a better time to come. That time would be characterized by justice, order and righteousness, and the nation would be respected by the world. But the later views changed somewhat in reference to this future, and are found in the extra-canonical books. The vision was expanded to the world, all of which was to be embraced in a wide-stretching kingdom under Israel and the Messiah as the representatives of God. This development was rapid in the two or three centuries preceding the Christian era. The hopes of the Maccabean patriots included little more than victory to the saints. There was here revealed, as shown in the book of Daniel, the idea of the nation rather than the personal Messiah as victor. In Ecclesiasticus, Judith, 2 Maccabees, and Tobit, the heathen are to be judged, and Israel delivered and gathered again into a national life which is to last forever under a Davidic king. Jerusalem shall be rebuilt in glory, and the heathen converted to the true faith. In the Sibyllines the picture is that of a great king fighting a battle with the kings of the world, who are to perish. God's people shall be blessed, and other nations shall serve them, bringing gifts. Jerusalem is to be the center and capital of the world. In Enoch there is expected an attack of heathen; but God will be victorious, and then judgment will be pronounced on fallen angels and apostate Jews. The New Jerusalem will be built and Messiah will appear as ruler. Thus the hope took on later and more fantastic phases, till it is not strange that in the time of Jesus the popular idea was that of a temporal king, who should wage war on the national enemies, and restore political liberty to Israel. But the true picture of the Messianic King and Servant is found in the pages of the Old Testament painted as on a canvas. Beside that picture Jesus stood one day, and pointing to it, said to the Jews, "Ye search the Scriptures, for in them ye think ye have eternal life; and these are they which bear witness of me. But ye will not come to me that ye may have life" (John 5:39, 40).

QUESTIONS

1. What was Israel's relation to God and to the world? What was the character of its selection? Was the nation as a whole able to accomplish its mission? What was necessary? 2. What is the significance of the words "Messiah" and "Messianic"? What prophet first described the work of the Messiah? In what terms? In what prophecy does the description of the Messiah as a suffering servant appear? By what process was the conception of the servant narrowed and exalted to the Messiah? 3. What, therefore, is the character of Messianic prophecy? In what sense may certain events or statements of the Old Testament be said to find their fulfillment in the life of Christ? What were the later Jewish ideas regarding the Messiah, and in what books do they appear? What did Jesus say of the Old Testament and of the Jewish attitude toward Him as the Messiah?

BIBLIOGRAPHY

THE HISTORY OF ISRAEL

Kent, C. F.—History of the Hebrew People, 2 vols. (Scribners), $1.25 per vol.
Kent, C. F.—History of the Jewish People (Scribners), $1.25.
Kittel, R.—History of the Hebrews, 2 vols. (Williams & Norgate), $1.50 per vol.
McCurdy, J. F.—History, Prophecy and the Monuments, 3 vols. (Macmillan), $3.00 per vol.
Stanley, A. P.—Lectures on the History of the Jewish Church, 3 vols (Scribners), $1.50 per vol.
Consult also, under the appropriate heads, the various encyclopædias and Bible Dictionaries, especially the Encyclopædia Britannica, 9th ed., and Hastings' Bible Dictionary.

GENERAL WORKS ON PROPHECY

Kirkpatrick, A. F.—The Doctrine of the Prophets.
Orelli—Old Testament Prophecy.
Smith, W. R.—The Prophets of Israel.
Cornill, C. H.—The Prophets of Israel.
Briggs, C. A.—Messianic Prophecy.
Ewald—The Prophets of the Old Testament.
Ottley, R. L.—The Hebrew Prophets.
Sanders and Kent—Messages of the Earlier Prophets; Messages of the Later Prophets.
The various prophetic books in the Cambridge Bible for Schools and Colleges.

THE PROPHETIC BOOKS

Isaiah—Driver (Men of the Bible), G. A. Smith, 2 vols., (Expositor's Bible), Cheyne, Delitzsch, Moulton.
Jeremiah—Cheyne (Men of the Bible), Bennett (Expositor's Bible), Moulton.
Ezekiel—Davidson (Cambridge Bible), Moulton.
Daniel.—Farrar (Expositor's Bible), Beven, Pusey.
The Minor Prophets—Farrar (Men of the Bible), G. A. Smith, 2 vols., (Expositor's Bible), Dods (Post-Exilian Prophets), Moulton.

CHRONOLOGICAL TABLE.

First Period: Moses to Solomon.

Moses, c. 1350 B. C.   Samuel, c. 1050 B. C.   David, 1017-977 B. C.
Nathan, Gad.
Solomon, 977-937 B. C.   Ahijah of Shiloh.

Second Period: Israel and Judah.

Kings of Israel.	Prophets of Israel	Kings of Judah	Prophets of Judah	Contemporary Events
Jeroboam I., 937		Rehoboam, 937		
		Abijam, 920		
Nadab, 915		Asa, 917		
Baasha, 913				
Elah, 889				
Zimri, 889				
Omri, 887		Jehoshaphat, 876		
Ahab, 875	Elijah			
Ahaziah, 853		Jehoram, 851		
Joram, 851		Ahaziah, 843		
Jehu, 842	Elisha	Athaliah, 842		Israel's wars with Syria. Jehu pays tribute to Shalm. II. of Assyria
		Joash, 836		
Jehoahaz, 814				
Jehoash, 797		Amaziah, 796		
Jeroboam II., 781	Jonah Amos Hosea	Azariah (Uzziah), 782		Tiglath-pileser III. of Assyria (745-727)
Zechariah, 740				
Shallum, 740				
Menahem, 740				
Pekahiah, 737		Jotham, 737	Isaiah (737-701)	Syro-Ephraimitish War
Pekah, 735		Ahaz, 735	Micah	Shalm. IV. (727-722)
Hoshea, 724				Sargon, (722-705)
(Fall of Samaria, 721 B. C.)				
		Hezekiah, 715		Sennacherib, (705-681)
		Manasseh, 686		
		Amon, 641	Nahum	
		Josiah, 639	Zephaniah	
		Finding of law-book. Great reformation, 721	Habakkuk Jeremiah (627-577)	Fall of Nineveh, 607
		Jehoahaz, 609		
		Jehoiakim, 609		Nebuchadrezzar (605-562)
		Jehoiachin, 597		
		Zedekiah, 597		
		(Fall of Jerusalem, 586)		

155

Third Period: The Exile and the Revival of Judah.

Leading Events	Prophetic Work	Contemporary Events
First deportation to Babylon, 597 Fall of Jerusalem, 586	Daniel Obadiah Ezekiel (592–567) *Isaiah 40-66* (?) 550-538)	
Edict of Cyrus permitting Jews to return, 538. First Return, under Sheshbazzar, 537 Return under Jerubbabel and Joshua, Temple begun, 534		Conquest of Babylon b; Cyrus of Persia, 538
Temple completed, 516. Nehemiah governor, 445-432. Ezra's expedition(?) 397	Haggai and Zechariah, 520 *Malachi* (?) Joel (?) *Book of Jonah* (?)	Darius I., 521-485 Xerxes I., 485-464 Artaxerxes I., 464-424 Artaxerxes II., 404-358
Maccabean uprising, 166.	*Zechariah 9-14* (?) *Book of Daniel* (?)	Wars of Alexander, 333-32 Rival kingdoms of Syri and Egypt, 322-200 Antiochus Epiphanes, 176-1:

www.ingramcontent.com/pod-product-compliance
Lightning Source LLC
Chambersburg PA
CBHW030336170426
43202CB00010B/1142